Learn French for Beginners

An Easy and Fast Way to Learn the Basics of French Language, Build Your Vocabulary, and Improve Your Reading and Conversation Skills

Table of Contents

Introduction

Having the ability to communicate in more than one language is practical for both business and pleasure. It enables you to effectively converse with people from different cultural backgrounds and provides you with unique experiences. In order to do that, you may want to have a valuable crash course in French.

Take note: this book will not make you fluent in French within weeks nor does it offer a means to understand the language without exerting much effort. Learning a new language requires time and dedication from your side. What this book promises is an effective way to learn French.

The first half of this book deals with the basics of French grammar. It defines the different elements of the language, their functions, and how you should use them. These concepts are described in such a way that beginners can easily understand them and grammar rules are explained using numerous examples.

You can treat the second half as a mini-dictionary and phrase book that will allow you to grow your vocabulary and speak some French while you're becoming proficient at grammar. The words and expressions listed in this book are helpful for everyday use and travel to French-speaking regions.

Finally, each chapter in this book ends with a set of exercises that will help you gauge your understanding of the language.

Thanks for purchasing this book. I hope you enjoy it!

Chapter 1: Learning the Basics

The French Alphabet and Pronunciation

The French language uses the same alphabet as the English language. While many of the letters are pronounced exactly the same, the vowels in particular sound rather different in French.

Consonants

The letters *b, d, f, k, l, m, n, p, s, t, v,* and *z* have the same pronunciation as in English if they occur at the beginning or middle of a word. Except for *l*, these letters are generally not pronounced when they occur at the end of a word.

bien	*byaN*	well
lundi	*luhN-dee*	Monday
devant	*duh-vahN*	in front of

Pronunciation Guide

Letter	Symbol	Pronunciation	Examples
c - before *a, o, u,* or a consonant final q	k	Say **c** as in **cold.**	cravate **k**rah-vaht (tie) escale ehs-**k**ahl (stopover)
c - before *e, i, h,* or *y*	s	Say **c** as in **center.**	glace glahs (mirror)

ç s – beginning of word or next to another consonant			prochain *proh-shahN* (next) garcon *gahr-sohN* (boy) sortie *sohr-tee* (exit) est *ehst* (east)
g – before *a, o, u,* or a consonant gu – before *i, e,* or *y*	g	Say **g** as in **goal**.	grand *grahN* (big) guichet *gee-sheh* (ticket window)
g – before *e, i,* or *y* ge – before *a* or *o* j	zh	Say **s** as in **treasure**.	imaginative *ee-mah-zhee-nah-teef* (imaginative) étage *ay-tahzh* (floor) jupe *zhewp* (skirt)
h *	-	Never pronounced.	hiver *ee-vehr* (winter)
r *	r	No equivalent. *	robe *rohb* (dress)
s – between vowels or followed by -	z	Say **z** as in **zoo**.	chemise *shuh-meez* (shirt)

3

ion			television *tay-lay-vee-zyohN* (tv)
x – followed by consonant or followed by a vowel at the end of a word	ks	Say **xc** as in **excellent.**	taxe *tah**ks*** (tax)
x - beginning of a word or between two vowels in separate syllables	gz	Say **gz** as in **example.**	exemple *eh**g**-zahNpl* (example)

*Note:

- The letter *h* is either a vowel (*h-muet*) or consonant (*h-aspiré*) in French. Distinguishing between the two is important when applying elision and liaison. Unfortunately, there's no rule that will help you identify which is considered a vowel or consonant. The only way to do this is by consulting a French dictionary.

- The sound of French *r* doesn't have an English equivalent. The English *r* is pronounced in the central part of the mouth while the French *r* is pronounced at the back of the throat. To say *r*, open your mouth and close your throat as if you're going to say the sound of *k*. Rest your tongue at the bottom of your mouth and against your teeth. Clear your throat and try saying *ra* at the same time.

The general rule is that a word's final consonant is not pronounced unless it ends with c, r, f, and l. Although this is the norm, there are a few notable exceptions.

- The final consonant of the following words is not pronounced.

banc	*bahN*	bench
blanc	*blahN*	white
estomac	*ehs-toh-mah*	stomach
franc	*frahN*	frank
gentil	*zhahN-tee*	kind
nerf	*nehr*	nerve
outil	*ooh-tee*	tool
porc	*pohr*	pork
tabac	*tah-bah*	tobacco

- The final consonant of the following words is neither c, f, l, or r but it should be pronounced.

as	*ahs*	ace
cap	*kahp*	cape
coq	*kohk*	rooster

fils	*fees*	son
maïs	*mah-ees*	corn
net	*neht*	clear
oust	*wehst*	west
sud	*sewd*	south

- The final *x* is never pronounced except in these two words where it takes the sound of *s*.

dix	*dees*	ten
six	*sees*	six

- The final consonant of foreign words adopted by the French language, like **internet** and **sandwich**, should always be pronounced

Vowels

Vowels used in the French language are more complicated than their English counterparts. Each one can have a number of distinct sounds. There are specific rules that will help you determine how vowels should be pronounced. Accent marks will also guide you in speaking French properly.

Five accent marks are used in the French alphabet – four are applied to vowels while only one is used on a consonant. Accent marks change the pronunciation of a letter and are used to distinguish two words with different meanings but are spelled the same way.

- The accent *aigu* (´) is only added on an *e* (é) and produces the sound of *ay* as in *may*.

- The accent *circonflexe* (ˆ) can be added on all vowels. The sounds of *â* and *ô* are distinctly longer while that of *ê* is slightly longer. Changes in the sounds of *î* and *û* are slight.

- The accent *grave* (`) can be added on *a, e,* or *u* but only *a* (à) produces a different sound.

- The *trema* is used when two vowels occur in a series. It is placed on the second vowel to indicate that the two should be pronounced separately.

- The *cédille* (ˌ) is only added to a *c* to form *ç* which produces the sound of *s*.

Pronunciation Guide

Letter	Symbol	Pronunciation	Examples
a à â	ah	Say **a** as in **far**.	avant **ah-vahN** (before) déjà *day-zhah* (already) gâteau *gah-to* (cake)
e* – when followed by one consonant in the middle of a	uh	Say **e** as in **the.**	ce *suh* (this, that) reçu *ruh-sew* (receipt)

word or when in a one-syllable word			
é	ay	Say **ay** as in **may.**	météo *may-tay-o* (weather) église *ay-gleez* (church)
è ê e – followed by a final pronounced consonant or two consonants	eh	Say **e** as in **pet.**	mère *mehr* (mother) être *ehtr* (to be) mer *mehr* (sea) rester *rehs-tay* (to stay)
i î y*	ee	Say **i** as in **machine**.	joli *zhoh-lee* (pretty) dîner *dee-nay* (dinner) y *ee* (there)
o – before *se* o – last pronounced sound of a word	o	Say **o** as in **cold.**	rose *roz* (pink) metro *may-tro* (subway) tôt *to* (early)

ô			
o – followed by a pronounced consonant sound	oh	Say **o** as in **ton.**	bol *bohl* (bowl)
u * û	ew	No equivalent.	tu *tew* (you) brûlure *brew-lewr* (burn)

Notes:

- For words ending in *consonant + e*, the final letter *e* is usually not pronounced unless it's a two-letter word.

- In the French alphabet, *y* is considered a vowel.

- Just like the letter *r*, the sound of the French *u* doesn't exist in English. To pronounce the *u* in French, try saying the *ue* in *true* but purse your lips tightly as if you're saying *ee* in *tree*.

Letter Combinations

Combined letters - whether a vowel sequence, two consonants, or vowel and consonant(s) - produce sounds that are quite different from the sounds of individual letters. In addition, when a single *m* or *n* follows a vowel and they are in the same syllable, the vowel sound should be followed by a nasal *n*.

Pronunciation Guide

Letter	Symbol	Pronunciation	Examples
er – final sound ez es – in some single-syllable words et (word)	ay	Say **a** as in **may.**	aimer *eh-**may*** (to love, like) nez n***ay*** (nose) des *d**ay*** (from) et ***ay*** (and)
ai – with a few exceptions* ei et	eh	Say **e** as in **pet.**	faire *f**eh**r* (to do, make) beignet *b**eh**-ny**eh*** (doughnut)
eu	uh	Say **e** as in **the.**	seulement *s**uh**l-mahN* (only)
ill*, il - preceded by a vowel	y	Say **y** as in **year.**	travailler *trah-vah-**y**ay* (to work) soleil *soh-leh**y*** (sun)
au eau	o	Say **o** as in **cold.**	chaussettes *sho-seht* (socks) bateau *bah-**to*** (boat)

oi oy	wah	Say **w** as in **water**.	mois *mwah* (month) voyager *vwah-yah-zhay* (to travel)
ou où oû	oo	Say **oo** as in **booth**.	poulet *poo-let* (chicken) où *oo* (where) goûter *goo-tay* (early afternoon snack)
gn	ny	Say **n** as in **onion**.	champagne *shahN-pah-nyuh* (champagne)
qu	k	Say **c** as in **cold.**	que *kuh* (that, what)
th*	t	Say **t** as in **ten**.	thé *tay* (tea)
Nasal Sounds			
am, an em, en	ahN	Similar to the word **on**.	jambon *zhahN-bohN* (ham) prendre *prahNdr* (to take)
aim, ain im, in	aN	Similar to the word **an**.	faim *faN* (hunger) impermeable *aN-*

			pehr-may-ahbl (raincoat)
ien	yaN	Similar to **yan** of **Yank**.	bien *byaN* (well)
oin	waN	Similar to **wan** of **wand**.	loin *lwaN* (away, far)
om, on	ohN	Similar to **on** in **long**.	monter *mohN-tay* (to go up)
um, un	uhN	Similar to **un** of **under**.	brun *bruhN* (brown)

Notes:

- Although *ill* is usually pronounced as *y*, there are a few exceptions:

  - mille *meel* (thousand)

  - million *mee-lyohN* (million)

  - tranquille *trahN-keel* (tranquil)

  - ville *veel* (city, town)

  - village *vee-lahzh* (village)

- The French language has no *th* sound.

Liaison and Elision

Liaison and elision are two elements of the French language. Because the boundaries between French syllables or words are not clear, these two linguistic elements facilitate the link between words and give language fluidity.

Liaison

When a word ending in a consonant is followed by a word that begins with a vowel or *h*, the final consonant is linked with the initial vowel. Through this linking or liaison, the consonant, which is usually silent, gets pronounced at the start of the word that follows.

Liaison does not affect how these words are spelled or written. However, some consonants change their sounds when used in liaisons.

- Final -*s* or -*x* is pronounced as z.

    o vous arrivez - *voo zah-ree-vay*

    o aux enfants - *o zahNfahN*

- Final -*d* or -*t* is pronounced as t.

    o un grand hôtel – *uhn-grahN-to-tehl*

    o petit ami – *puh-tee-tah-mee*

- Final nasal -*n* or -*m* loses the nasal sound at the beginning of the following word.

    o mon ami – *mohN nah-mee*

- When linked with *ans* or *heures*, the final -*f* or *neuf* takes a v sound.

    o neuf ans – *nuh vahN*

○ neuf heures – *nuh vuhr*

Liaisons are either mandatory or optional. However, not all final consonants and initial vowels should be linked. These are the cases where liaison is prohibited:

- After the word *et*

- After proper names

- After singular nouns

- Before the word *onze*

- The second word begins with *h-aspiré*

- The first word is a noun and the second is an adjective

- The first word is a plural noun and the second is a verb

- The first word is either *ils, elles,* or *on* and the second is a past-participle

Elision

This occurs between two words when the ending of the first and the beginning of the next are pronounced vowel sounds. In contrast with liaison, elision or sliding affects how the words are written. In particular, the final vowel of the first word is replaced by an apostrophe.

○ le + animal – l'animal

○ ce + est – c'est

○ la + haleine – l'haleine

○ je + arrive – j'arrive

Elision is almost always mandatory. However, there are also a few exceptions where elision shouldn't be used.

- After the word *qui*

- Before the words *onze* and *oui*

- Before a word that begins with *h-aspiré*

- Between the words *la* and *une*

- Before nouns that begin with the letter *y*

Stress

In English, stress can fall on any syllable depending on the word itself. In French, you can easily predict the stress or *l'accentuation* because it is always placed on the last syllable of a word. You should give all the other syllables equal emphasis and the final syllable a slightly stronger stress.

  o Cana**dian** – canadi**en**

  o Medite**rra**nean – Méditerran**ee**

  o **Pa**ris – **Pa**ris

When you say a phrase or sentence, you should only emphasize the last syllable of the last word. Because French speakers consider a string of words as one word, all the other words lose their stress.

Numbers

We use numbers every single day of our lives. Aside from counting, we use them to tell the time and date or express our age. Therefore, one of the most basic things that you should learn is how to count in French.

Cardinal Numbers

These are whole numbers that we use to count and indicate quantity. Although numbers are basically infinite, you don't need to memorize thousands of words. You only have to learn a few words and then repeat or combine them with others to form the words for larger numbers.

Consider the numbers from 1 to 10 as base numbers.

0	zéro	*zay-ro*
1	un	*uhN*
2	deux	*duh*
3	trois	*trwah*
4	quatre	*kahtr*
5	cinq	*saNk*
6	six	*sees*
7	sept	*seht*
8	huit	*weet*
9	neuf	*nuhf*
10	dix	*dees*

The numbers from 11 to 16 are similar to the numbers from 1 to 6. Note that -*ze* is added after some spelling changes.

11	onze	*ohNz*
12	douze	*dooz*
13	treize	*trehz*
14	quatorze	*kah-tohrz*
15	quinze	*kaNz*
16	seize	*sehz*

For 17 to 19, *dix* (ten) is combined with one of the base numbers. Note that when you combine these numbers, they are joined by a hyphen and treated as one word.

17	dix-sept	*dee-seht*
18	dix-huit	*dee-zweet*
19	dix-neuf	*dee-nuhf*

Memorize the multiples of ten from 20 to 60. For the numbers 21, 31, 41, 51, and 61, combine them with *un* (one) using the conjunction *et* (and). To form the other numbers, join the tens and the base numbers (2 to 9) with a hyphen.

20	vingt	*vaN*
21	vingt et un	*vaN-tay-uhN*
22	vingt-deux	*vaN-duh*

23	vingt-troix	*vaN- trwah*
24	vingt-quatre	*vaN- kahtr*
25	vingt-cinq	*vaN-saNk*
26	vingt-six	*vaN-sees*
27	vingt-sept	*vaN-seht*
28	vingt-huit	*vaN-weet*
29	vingt-neuf	*vaN-nuhf*
30	trente	*trahNt*
31	trente et un	*trahN-tay-uhN*
32	trente-deux	*trahNt-duh*
33	trente-troix	*trahNt-trwah*
40	quarante	*kah-rahNt*
44	quarante-quatre	*kah-rahNt-kahtr*
45	quarante-cinq	*kah-rahNt-saNk*
50	cinquante	*saN-kahNt*
56	cinquante-six	*saN-kahNt-sees*
57	cinquante-sept	*saN-kahNt-seht*
60	soixante	*swah-sahNt*
68	soixante-huit	*swah-sahNt-weet*
69	soixante-neuf	*swah-sahNt-nuhf*

The French word for 70 is a combination of 60 and 10. You're literally adding these joined numbers. To form the next nine numbers (71 to 79), combine 60 with the numbers from 11 to 19.

70	soixante-dix	*swah-sahNt-dees*
71	soixante et onze	*swah-sahNt-ay-ohNz*
72	soixante-douze	*swah-sahNt-dooz*
73	soixante-treize	*swah-sahNt-trehz*
74	soixante-quatorze	*swah-sahNt-kah-tohrz*
75	soixante-quinze	*swah-sahNt-kaNz*
76	soixante-seize	*swah-sahNt-sehz*
77	soixante-dix-sept	*swah-sahNt-dee-seht*
78	soixante-dix-huit	*swah-sahNt-dee-zweet*
79	soixante-dix-neuf	*swah-sahNt-dee-nuhf*

The French word for 80 literally translates to four-twenties. And when you have four 20's, you get 80.

You can form the numbers from 81 to 99 by combining the numbers 1 to 19 with 80. Note that for 81 and 91, *un* and *onze* are joined by a hyphen and not the word *et*.

80	quatre-vingts	*kahtr-vaN*
81	quatre-vingt-un	*kahtr-vaN-uhN*
82	quatre-vingt-deux	*kahtr-vaN-duh*
83	quatre-vingt-trois	*kahtr-vaN-trwah*
84	quatre-vingt-quatre	*kathr-vaN- kahtr*
85	quatre-vingt-cinq	*kathr-vaN-saNk*
90	quatre-vingt-dix	*kahtr-vaN-dees*
91	quatre-vingt-onze	*kahtr-vaN-onze*
96	quatre-vingt-seize	*kahtr-vaN-sehz*
97	quatre-vingt- dix-sept	*kahtr-vaN-dee-seht*
98	quatre-vingt- dix-huit	*kahtr-vaN-dee-zweet*
99	quatre-vingt-dix-neuf	*kahtr-vaN-dee-nuhf*

The French word for 100 is *cent*. To form the succeeding numbers, combine it with the numbers from 1 to 99 but don't add a hyphen or *et* after *cent*.

100	cent	*sahN*
101	cent un	*sahN-uhN*
102	cent deux	*sahN-duh*

110	cent dix	*sahN-dee*
121	cent vingt et un	*sahN- vaN-tay-uhN*
156	cent cinquante-six	*sahN-saN-kahNt-sees*

To form the multiples of 100, combine the base numbers 2 to 9 with *cents*.

200	deux cents	*duh-sahN*
300	trois cents	*trwah-sahN*
400	quatre cents	*kahtr-sahN*

Drop the final *s* in *cents* and follow the same rule for 101 to 199 to form the other numbers.

531	cinq cent trente et un	*saNk-sahN-trahN-tay-uhN*
650	six cent cinquante	*sees-sahN- saN-kahNt*
799	sept cent quatre-vingt-dix-neuf	*seht-sahN- kahtr-vaN-dee-nuhf*

The French word for thousand is *mille*. Like cent, a hyphen or the word *et* is not added when it's joined with other numbers. However, *mille* doesn't take an *s* when forming the multiples of one thousand.

1000	mille	*meel*
1001	mille un	*meel-uhN*
1200	mille deux cents	*meel-duh-sahN*
2000	deux mille	*duh-meel*
3000	trois mille	*trwah-meel*

Finally, here are the French words for numbers beyond thousands.

1,000,000	un million	*uhN-meel-yohN*
2,000,000	deux millions	*duh-meel-yohN*
1,000,000,000	un milliard	*uhN-meel-yahr*
2,000,000,000	deux milliards	*duh-meel-yahr*
one trillion	un billion	*uhN-beel-yohN*
one quadrillion	un billiard	*uhN-beel-yahr*

Ordinal Numbers

Although the use of ordinal numbers in day-to-day conversations is less frequent than that of cardinal numbers, they are still quite useful. If you want to express things in order, you will need to use ordinal numbers.

Now that you know your cardinal numbers, it will be easy to learn the ordinal numbers. As you can see from the table below, ordinal numbers are formed by adding the suffix -*ième* to the cardinal number, with a few exceptions.

English	French	*Pronunciation*
first	premier / première	*pruh-myay / pruh-myehr*
second	deuxième / second(e)	*duh-zyehm / suh-gohN(d)*
third	troisième	*trwah-zyehm*
fourth	quatrième	*kah-tree-yehm*
fifth	cinquième	*saN-kyehm*
sixth	sixième	*see-zyehm*
seventh	septième	*seh-tyehm*
eighth	huitième	*wee-tyehm*
ninth	neuvième	*nuh-vyehm*
10th	dixième	*dee-zyehm*
11th	onzième	*ohN-zyehm*
12th	douzième	*doo-zyehm*
13th	treizième	*treh-zyehm*
14th	quatorzième	*kah-tohr-zyehm*
15th	quinzième	*kaN-zyehm*
16th	seizième	*seh-zyehm*
17th	dix-septième	*dee-seh-tyehm*

18th	dix-huitième	*dee-zwee-tyehm*
19th	dix-neuvième	*dee-nuh-vyehm*
20th	vingtième	*vaN-tyehm*
21st	vingt et unième	*vaN-tay-uhN-nyehm*
30th	trentième	*trahN-tyehm*
100th	centième	*sahN-tyehm*

Aside from *premier* for first, here are other exceptions:

- Numbers ending in -e such as *quatre* and *trente* drop the final -e before adding the suffix.

- The suffix for the number *cinq* and all its variations is -*uième*.

- The number *neuf* and all its variations replaces the final -*f* with -*v* before adding the suffix.

- If there's no third in a series, *second(e)* is used instead of *deuxième*.

Note that only *premier* and *second* have to agree with the gender of the noun they modify.

Telling Time

Now that you've learned French numbers, you can easily express time and respond to, *Quelle heure est-il?* (What time is it?)

To answer the above question, the following words and expressions will be quite useful:

time	l'heure	*luhr*
noon	midi	*mee-dee*
midnight	minuit	*mee-nwee*
and a half	et demie	*ay-duh-mee*
quarter to	moins le quart	*mwaN-luh-kahr*
and a quarter	et quart	*ay-kahr*
in the morning or a.m	du matin	*dew-mah-taN*
in the afternoon or p.m.	de l'après-midi	*day-lah-preh-mee-dee*
in the evening/night	du soir	*dew-swah*

- To express time on the hour, use *il est* + number + *heure(s)*. While we often leave out the expression o'clock when telling time in English, you always need to use its French equivalent, which is *heure(s)*.

  o Il est une heure. / It's 1:00.

  o Il est cinq heures. / It's 5:00.

- If the number of minutes after the hour is less than 30, simply add that number to the previous expression.

  o Il est deux heures cinq. / It's 2:05

- o   Il est troix heures vingt-cinq. / It's 3:25.

- If the number of minutes after the hour is more than 30, express time before the hour using *moins* (before, minus).

  - o   Il est neuf heures moins dix. / It's 8:50. (It's 10 minutes before 9.)

  - o   It est quatre heures moins vingt. / It's 3:40. (It's 20 minutes before 4.)

- Use *demie* and *midi* to express 15, 30, and 45 minutes.

  - o   Il est quatre heures et quart. / It's 4:15.

  - o   Il est sept heures et demie. / It's 7:30.

  - o   Il est dix heures moins le quart. / It's 9:45.

- Follow the examples below to express time relative to noon and midnight.

  - o   Il est midi (minuit). / It's noon (midnight).

  - o   Il est midi (minuit) et demi. / It's half past noon (midnight).

  - o   Il est midi moins cinq. / It's 11:55 a.m.

  - o   Il est minuit dix. / It's 12:05 a.m.

12-hr vs. 24-hr clock

In French, the 24-hr clock is more commonly used than the 12-hr clock. But don't worry. Expressing time using this system is the same. Look at the following examples:

- Il est dix-sept heures. / It's 17:00 (5:00 p.m.).

- Il est treize heures vingt-cinq. / It's 13:25 (1:25 p.m.).

- Il est vingt heures et demie. / It's 20:30 (8:30 p.m.).

- Il est quatorze heures moins le quart. / Its 13:45 (1:45 p.m.).

Writing time in numerical form is different in English and French. Time expressed using the 12-hr system also differs from that of the 24-hr clock.

- 12-hour clock – 4h25

- 24-hour clock – 18.30

Expressing Date

To talk about dates, you use numbers. However, you also need to know the names of days and months. Note that the names of days and months are always written in lowercase unless they're used at the beginning of a sentence.

English	French	*Pronunciation*
day	jour	*zhoor*
Monday	lundi	*luhN-dee*
Tuesday	mardi	*mahr-dee*
Wednesday	mercredi	*mehr-kruh-dee*
Thursday	jeudi	*zhuh-dee*

Friday	vendredi	*vahN-druh-dee*
Saturday	samedi	*sahm-dee*
Sunday	dimanche	*dee-mahNsh*
month	mois	*mwah*
January	janvier	*zhahN-vee-yay*
February	février	*fay-vree-yay*
March	mars	*mahrs*
April	avril	*ah-vreel*
May	mai	*meh*
June	juin	*zhwaN*
July	juillet	*zhwee-eh*
August	août	*oo(t)*
September	septembre	*sehp-tahNbr*
October	octobre	*ohk-tohbr*
November	novembre	*noh-vahNbr*
December	décembre	*day-sahNbr*

To express the date in French, follow the pattern below:

name of day + *le* + cardinal number + name of month + year

- mardi le 08 octobre 2019

Note that cardinal numbers are used to express a specific date except for the first day of the month. In this case, you will have to use the abbreviation for *premier* which is *1er*.

Writing the date using numerical abbreviation in French is also different compared to how it's done by English speakers. Instead of starting with the month, the day is written first.

- English: 11/30/2019

- French: 30/11/2019

Cognates

Cognates are your friends. If you know how to identify them, you can easily widen your French vocabulary.

Cognates result from borrowing of words. In some cases, the English language borrowed from the French. In others, the French borrowed from English. These words can have the same or similar spelling. While the pronunciation is almost always different, cognates have exactly the same meaning.

Perfect Cognates

These are cognates that have no difference in spelling. French words with the following endings are perfect cognates.

Word Ending	French	Pronunciation
-al (but not -ical)	animal	*ah-nee-mahl*
	final	*fee-nahl*
	mental	*mahN-tahl*
	original	*oh-ree-zhee-nahl*

-ance	ambulance	*ahN-bew-lahNs*
	distance	*dees-tahNs*
	finance	*fee-nahNs*
	substance	*sewbs-tahNs*
-ble	adorable	*ah-doh-rahbl*
	horrible	*oh-reebl*
	possible	*poh-seebl*
	table	*tahbl*
-tion	conversation	*kohN-vehr-sah-syohN*
	information	*een-fohr-mah-syohN*
	station	*stah-syohN*
	tradition	*trah-dee-syohN*
-ent	accident	*ahk-see-dahN*
	client	*klee-yahN*
	permanent	*pehr-mah-nahN*
	content	*kohN-tahN*
-ct	correct	*koh-rehk*
	direct	*dee-rehk*
	impact	*ahN-pahk*
	respect	*rehs-pehk*
-ence	absence	*ahb-sahNs*

	patience	*pah-syahNs*
	science	*syahNs*
	violence	*vyoh-lahNs*

Here are other perfect cognates that do not follow any rule regarding word endings.

English-French Cognates	Pronunciation
accord	*ah-kohr*
active	*ahk-teev*
ballet	*bah-leh*
blond	*blohN*
blouse	*blooz*
bureau	*bew-ro*
certain	*sehr-taN*
chef	*shehf*
date	*daht*
dispute	*dees-pewt*
effective	*eh-fehk-teev*
fruit	*frwee*
gallon	*gah-lohN*
hotel	*o-tehl*

immense	*ee-mahNs*
impression	*ahN-preh-syohN*
note	*noht*
omelette	*ohm-leht*
orange	*oh-rahnzh*
route	*root*
soda	*soh-dah*

Near-Perfect Cognates

These cognates are spelled nearly the same in both English and French. Some of these cognates follow a pattern regarding word endings although the majority of them don't.

- English words that end in -ary change to -aire in French.

anniversary	anniversaire	*ah-nee-vehr-sehr*
dictionary	dictionnaire	*deek-syoh-nehr*
ordinary	ordinaire	*ohr-dee-nehr*
salary	salaire	*sah-lehr*
vocabulary	vocabulaire	*voh-kah-bew-lehr*

- English words that end in -ist usually change to -iste in French.

artist	artiste	*ahr-teest*
dentist	dentist	*dahN-teest*
pessimist	pessimiste	*peh-see-meest*
tourist	touriste	*too-reest*

- English words that end in -ical usually change to -ique in French.

critical	critique	*kree-teek*
electrical	électrique	*ay-lehk-treek*
logical	logique	*loh-zheek*
typical	typique	*tee-peek*

The following table lists more near-perfect cognates. Note that some of these words follow the rules for perfect cognates and are almost perfect except for slight changes in their vowels.

English	French	Pronunciation
actor	acteur	*ahk-tuhr*
address	adresse	*ah-drehs*
age	âge	*ahzh*
American	américain	*ah-may-ree-kaN*

apartment	appartement	*ah-pahr-tuh-mahN*
baby	bébé	*bay-bay*
blue	bleu	*bluh*
calculator	calculatrice	*kahl-kew-lah-trees*
Catholic	catholique	*kah-toh-leek*
color	couleur	*koo-luhr*
debate	débat	*day-bah*
delicious	délicieux	*day-lee-syuh*
different	différent	*dee-fay-rahN*
dinner	dîner	*dee-nay*
dramatic	dramatique	*drah-mah-teek*
edition	édition	*ay-dee-syohN*
entire	entier	*ahN-tyay*
family	famille	*fah-mee-y*
frequent	fréquent	*fray-kahN*
gradual	graduel	*grah-dew-ehl*
horror	horreur	*oh-ruhr*
interesting	intéressant	*aN-tay-reh-sahN*
juvenile	juvénile	*zhew-vay-neel*

lamp	lampe	*lahNp*
liberty	liberté	*lee-behr-tay*
music	musique	*mew-zeek*
nervous	nerveux	*nehr-vuh*
number	nombre	*nohNbr*
painter	peintre	*pehntr*
paper	papier	*pah-pyay*
park	parc	*pahrk*
pharmacy	pharmacie	*fahr-mah-see*
popular	populaire	*poh-pew-lehr*
quality	qualité	*kah-lee-tay*
rich	riche	*reesh*
romantic	romantique	*roh-mahN-teek*
soup	soupe	*soop*
status	statut	*stah-tew*
telephone	téléphone	*tay-lay-fohn*
television	television	*tay-lay-vee-zyohn*
traditional	traditionnel	*trah-dee-syoh-nehl*
uncle	oncle	*ohNkl*

university	université	*ew-nee-vehr-see-tay*
vendor	vendeur	*vahN-duhr*
visitor	visiteur	*vee-see-tuhr*
vulnerable	vulnérable	*vewl-nay-rahbl*
zero	zéro	*zay-ro*

False Cognates

Not all words that look similar are cognates. Many are actually deceiving and could get you into trouble if you mistake them for friends. Here are some of the most common false cognates that you should be wary of.

False English Cognate	French Cognate	French Meaning
actually	actuellement	currently, presently
to aim	aimer	to like
to assist	assister	to attend
to attend	attendre	to wait for
to bless	blesser	to hurt
bras	bras	arm
chair	chair	flesh
coin	coin	corner

comment	comment	how
a demand	une demande	a request
deception	déception	disappointment
douche (obnoxious person or medical device)	douche	shower
entrée	entrée	appetizer / starter
eventually	éventuellement	possibly
gross	gros(se)	fat
journey	journée	day
library	librairie	bookstore
location	location	rental
money	monnaie	coin
pain	pain	bread
to pass (an exam)	passer (un examen)	to take an exam
patron	patron	boss
preservative	préservatif	condom
to rest	rester	to stay
rude	rude	harsh
sale	sale	dirty
to travel	travailler	to work

Exercises

A. Numbers

Translate the following words to French.

1. 15

2. 0

3. 89

4. 70

5. 1,000

6. 35

7. 125

8. 540

9. 18

10. 4

11. fourth

12. tenth

13. twentieth

14. first

15. seventh

16. It's 8:40 a.m.

17. It's midnight.

18. It's 14:30.

19. It's 3:00 p.m.

20. It's 20:15.

21. Wednesday

22. Sunday

23. January

24. May

25. October

B. Cognates

Indicate whether the following words are perfect, near-perfect, or false cognates. If it's not a perfect cognate, provide the English meaning.

1. adresse

2. touriste

3. entier

4. chair

5. actuellement

6. électrique

7. déception

8. lampe

9. librairie

10. certain

11. tradition

12. préservatif

13. sale

14. substance

15. délicieux

Answers

A.

1. quinze

2. zéro

3. quatre-vingt-neuf

4. soixante-dix

5. mille

6. trente-cinq

7. cent vingt-cinq

8. cinq cent quarante

9. dix-huit

10. quatre

11. quatrième

12. dixième

13. vingtième

14. premier / première

15. septième

16. Il est neuf heures moins vingt du matin.

17. Il est minuit.

18. Il est quatorze heures et demie.

19. Il est troix heures de l'après-midi.

20. Il est vingt et quart.

21. mercredi

22. dimanche

23. janvier

24. mai

25. octobre

B.

1. near-perfect, address

2. near-perfect, tourist

3. near-perfect, entire

4. false, flesh

5. false, currently

6. near perfect, electric

7. false, disappointment

8. near-perfect, lamp

9. false, bookstore

10. perfect

11. perfect

12. false, condom

13. false, dirty

14. perfect

15. near-perfect, delicious

Chapter 2: Grammar Rules – Nouns

Nouns are words that refer to people, things, places, or ideas. In both English and French, nouns have a number; they have singular and plural forms. But unlike in English, French nouns have a gender. It doesn't matter whether what a noun refers to has an actual gender. Everything from a person to inanimate objects and abstract ideas are classified as either masculine or feminine.

You'll still be understood even if you don't get the right gender and number as long as you use the correct word. However, both are quite important since you'll be using them later on to determine which pronoun and what form of verb and adjective to use along with a specific noun.

Gender

If you're speaking about people or any animate object which are either male or female, the noun's gender will be obvious. If you're referring to places, things, or ideas, noun identifiers and some patterns can help you identify a noun's gender.

Articles

French nouns are usually paired with short identifiers known as articles. These articles are either definite or indefinite. When you learn a new word, always memorize the article that comes with it so you can easily tell its gender. The table that follows shows noun identifiers for singular nouns.

	Masculine		Feminine	
definite: the	le (l')	*luh*	la (l')	*lah*
indefinite: a, an	un	*uhN*	une	*ewn*

Note: When *le* and *la* are paired with nouns that start with a vowel, both of them become *l'* due to elision. For that kind of nouns, it's best to learn their partner indefinite article to keep the gender from being a mystery.

Word Endings

In most cases, a noun's ending can effectively tell you whether it's masculine or feminine. However, you have to keep in mind that there are always some exceptions.

Masculine Nouns

Noun Ending	Example		
	French	Pronunciation	English
-acle	miracle	*mee-rahkl*	miracle
	oracle	*oh-rahkl*	oracle
	spectacle	*spehk-tahkl*	show
-age	étage	*ay-tahzh*	floor (story)
	garage	*gah-rahzh*	garage
	essorage	*eh-soh-rahzh*	spin-drying, wringing

-al	animal	*ah-nee-mahl*	animal
	journal	*zhoor-nahl*	newspaper
	bocal	*boh-kahl*	jar
-ant	gérant	*zhay-rahN*	manager
	gant	*gahN*	glove
	commerçant	*koh-mehr-sahN*	merchant
-eau	chapeau	*shah-po*	hat
	gâteau	*gah-to*	cake
	manteau	*mahN-to*	overcoat
-ège	collège	*koh-lehzh*	school
	piège	*pehzh*	trap
	privilège	*pree-vee-lehzh*	privilege
-er and -ier	escalier	*ehs-kah-lyay*	stair
	atelier	*ah-tuh-lyay*	studio
	hamburger	*ahN-bewr-gehr*	hamburger
-et	billet	*bee-yeh*	ticket
	guichet	*gee-sheh*	ticket window
	millet	*mee-yeh*	birdseed

-é	été	*ay-tay*	summer
	hypermarché	*ee-pehr-mahr-shay*	large supermarket
	café	*kah-fay*	coffee
-in, -ain	train	*traN*	train
	magasin	*mah-gah-zaN*	store
	pain	*paN*	bread
-isme	tourisme	*too-reez-muh*	tourism
	prisme	*preez-muh*	prism
	charisme	*sha-reez-muh*	charisma
-ent, -ment(s)	avertissement	*ah-vehr-tees-mahN*	warning
	aliments	*ah-lee-mahN*	food
	argent	*ahr-zhahN*	money, silver
-oir	comptoir	*kohN-twahr*	counter
	miroir	*meer-wahr*	mirror
	abattoir	*ah-bah-twahr*	slaughterhouse
-on	avion	*ah-vyohN*	airplane
	crayon	*kreh-yohN*	pencil
	citron	*see-trohN*	lemon

Feminine Nouns

Noun Ending	Example		
	French	Pronunciation	English
-ade	ambassade	*ahN-bah-sahd*	embassy
	escalade	*ehs-kah-lahd*	rock-climbing
	limonade	*lee-moh-nahd*	lemonade
-ale	cathédrale	*kah-tay-drahl*	cathedral
	escale	*ehs-kahl*	stopover
-ance, -anse	chance	*shahNs*	luck
	ordonnance	*ohr-doh-nahNs*	prescription
	quittance	*kee-tahNs*	receipt
-ence, -ense	dépense	*day-pahNs*	payment
	essence	*eh-sahNs*	gasoline
	prudence	*prew-dahNs*	attention
-ette, -tte	assiette	*ah-syeht*	dinner plate
	crevette	*kruh-veht*	shrimp
	étiquette	*ay-tee-keht*	identification tag
-eur	chaleur	*sha-luh*	warmth
	douleur	*doo-luhr*	pain

	valeur	*vah-luhr*	value
-ie	librairie	*lee-breh-ree*	bookstore
	pluie	*plwee*	rain
	sortie	*sohr-tee*	exit
-ison	conjugaison	*kohn-zhu-geh-zohN*	conjugation
	maison	*meh-zohN*	house
	raison	*reh-zohN*	reason
-sion	décision	*day-see-zyohN*	decision
	expression	*ehks-preh-syohN*	expression
	télévision	*tay-lay-vee-zyohN*	tv
-té	amabilité	*ah-mah-bee-lee-tay*	kindness
	identité	*ee-dahN-tee-tay*	identity
	université	*ew-nee-vehr-see-tay*	university
-tié	amitié	*ah-mee-tay*	friendship
	moitié	*mwah-tay*	half
	pitié	*pee-tay*	mercy
-tion	addition	*ah-dee-syohN*	addition

	climatisation	*klee-mah-tee-zah-syohN*	air conditioning
	conversation	*kohN-vehr-sah-syohn*	conversation

Categories

Based on the category or group that a word belongs to, you can predict the gender of French nouns.

These groups of nouns are generally masculine:

- Numbers and quantities:

    o   un million / a million

    o   un tiers / a third

    o   un quart / a quart

- Names of countries that don't end in -*e*

    o   le Brésil / Brazil

    o   le Japon / Japan

- Names of languages

    o   le français / French

    o   le russe / Russian

- Units of measure in the metric system

    o   un litre / a liter

    o   un gramme / a gram

- Names of trees

    - un pommier / apple tree

    - un chêne / oak tree

- Borrowed English nouns

    - le basketball

    - le whisky

- Names of metals

    - l'or / gold

    - le cuivre / copper

- Names of days, months, and seasons

winter	l'hiver	*lee-vehr*
spring	le printemps	*luh praN-tahN*
summer	l'été	*lay-tay*
fall / autumn	l'automme	*lo-tohn*

The following categories are generally feminine:

- Names of countries and continents that end in -*e*

    - la France

    - l'Afrique

- Names of fruits and vegetables that end in -*e*

- o une pomme / apple

- o une carotte / carrot

- Names of rivers

  - o la Seine

  - o l'Amazone

- Names of sciences

  - o la chimie / chemistry

  - o la géographie / geography

Gender Conversions

In some cases, you can make a masculine noun feminine by simply adding an -*e*. The extra letter at the end of the word may or may not affect the pronunciation. Consider the following examples:

- friend: ami (*ah-mee*) – amie (*ah-mee*)

- lawyer: avocat (*ah-vo-kah*) – avocate (*ah-vo-kaht*)

The masculine noun can also lose its fanal nasal sound in the feminine form.

- cousin: cousin (*koo-zaN*) – cousine (*koo-zeen*)

Many masculine nouns that refer to professions have feminine counterparts. The feminine endings usually sound quite different from the masculine.

Le (L'), Un		La (L'), Une		English
acteur	*ahk-tuhr*	actrice	*ahk-trees*	actor/actress
pharmacien	*fahr-mah-syN*	pharmacienne	*fahr-mah-syehn*	pharmacit
programmeur	*proh-grah-muhr*	programmeuse	*proh-grah-muhz*	programmer
patron	*pah-trohN*	patronne	*pah-trohn*	boss

Some nouns can be masculine and feminine because their spelling is the same in both genders. Their gender will depend on whom the speaker is referring to.

	Masculine	Feminine
artist	un artiste	une artiste
athlete	un athlète	une athlète
dentist	un dentiste	une dentiste
child	un enfant	une enfant
sick person	le malade	la malade
tourist	le touriste	la touriste

There are also a few nouns which are always masculine or always feminine.

Always Masculine		
le professeur	*luh-proh-feh-suhr*	teacher
le médecin	*luh-mayd-saN*	doctor
le bébé	*luh-bay-bay*	baby
l'entrepreneur	*lahN-treh-pruh-nuhr*	businessman
le sénateur	*luh-say-nah-tuhr*	senator
Always Feminine		
connaissance	*koh-neh-sahNs*	acquaintance
personne	*pehr-sohn*	person
vedette	*vuh-deht*	star
victime	*veek-teem*	victim

If you want to use these fixed gender nouns to refer to the other gender, add the word *homme* before the feminine noun or *femme* before the masculine noun.

- une femme entrepreneur – a businesswoman

- un homme victime – a male victim

Pesky Nouns

You may be familiar with homonyms in English. They are words with exactly the same spelling but their meanings are entirely different. In French, the meanings of these "homonyms" depend on whether they're used as a masculine or feminine noun.

French Word	Masculine Meaning	Feminine Meaning
barde	poet	armor for a horse
basque	Basque language	tails of a jacket
casse	robber, break-in	damage, breakages
cave	idiot	basement, cellar
chèvre	goat cheese	goat
chine	rice paper	second-hand or used trade
chose	contraption	thing
crème	coffee with cream	cream
crêpe	crepe material	thin pancake
diesel	diesel fuel	diesel vehicle
faux	fake	scythe
finale	finale (music)	final (sports)
geste	gesture	epic poem
guide	guidebook, tour guide	girl scout
livre	book	pound (weight and

		currency)
manche	handle	sleeve
mari	husband	marijuana
mort	dead body	death
mémoire	memo, report	memory
merci	thanks	mercy
mode	method, mood	fashion
moule	mold	mussel
office	office	pantry
orange	orange (color)	orange (fruit)
physique	physique	physics
poche	paperback (book)	pocket, pouch
poêle	stove	frying pan
politique	politician	policy, politics
poste	job, post	post office
rose	pink (color)	rose (flower)
somme	snooze	sum
tour	tour, turn	tower
vase	vase	mud, silt

Number

When you use a noun to refer to more than one person, thing, place, or idea, you should use its plural form. The article that goes with it should also be in the plural form. The plural forms of articles are the same for both masculine and feminine nouns. Therefore, they only indicate the number and not the gender.

Article	Feminine / Masculine	Pronunciation
the (definite)	les	*lay*
some (indefinite)	des	*day*

The Plural Form of Nouns

There are a few general rules that you should follow to form the plural of French nouns. The most common is by adding an -s to the singular form, just like in English.

English	Singular	Pronunciation	Plural	Pronunciation
book(s)	le livre	*luh-leevr*	les livres	*lay-leevr*
boy(s)	un garçon	*uhN-gahr-sohN*	des garçons	*day-gahr-sohN*
girl(s)	la fille	*lah-fee-y*	les filles	*lay-fee-y*
table(s)	le table	*luh-tahbl*	les tables	*lay-tahbl*

Remember that this final -s is not pronounced. As you can see from the above examples, it doesn't change the pronunciation of the word.

If the singular form of the noun ends in -s or -x, you don't have to add a final -s. The only thing you need to do is change the article.

English	Singular	Pronunciation	Plural	Pronunciation
bus(es)	l'autobus	*lo-toh-bews*	les autobus	*lay-zo-toh-bews*
arm(s)	le bras	*lu-brah*	les bras	*lay-brah*
cross(es)	la croix	*lah-krwah*	les croix	*lay-krwah*
voice(s)	la voix	*lah-vwah*	les voix	*lay-vwah*

The French language also uses the letter *x* to form the plural of a noun. These are irregular cases and there are always exceptions the rules.

- Add -*x* to singular nouns that end in -*eau,* -*eu,* and -*au.*

English	Singular	Pronunciation	Plural	Pronunciation
boat	le bâteau	*luh-bah-to*	les bâteaux	*lay-bah-to*
castle	le château	*luh-shah-to*	les châteaux	*lay-shah-to*
game	le jeu	*luh-zhuh*	les jeux	*lay-zhuh*

| bucket | le seau | *luh-so* | les seaux | *lay-so* |
| jewel | le bijou | *luh-bee-zhoo* | les bijoux | *lay-bee-zhoo* |

Exception:

- o tire: le pneu – les pneus

- Change the ending of masculine singular nouns from *-al* to *-aux*.

English	Singular	Pronunciation	Plural	Pronunciation
animal	l'animal	*lah-nee-mahl*	les animaux	*lay-zah-nee-mo*
journal	un journal	*uhN-zhoor-nahl*	des journaux	*day-zhoor-no*
cheval	les cheval	*lay-shuh-vahl*	les chevaux	*lay-shuh-vo*

Exceptions:

- o ball (dance): le bal – les bals

- o festival: le festival – les festivals

- o valley: le val – les vals

- The plural form of nouns ending in *-ou* normally ends in *-s*. The following are the exceptions:

le bijou	les bijoux	*lay-bee-zhoo*	jewel(s)
le chou	les choux	*lay-shoo*	cabbage(s)
le caillou	les cailloux	*lay-kah-yoo*	pebble(s)
le genou	les genoux	*lay-zhuh-noo*	knee(s)
le hibou	les hiboux	*lay-ee-boo*	owl(s)
le joujou	les joujoux	*lay-zhoo-zhoo*	toy(s)
le pou	les poux	*lay-poo*	louse/lice

- Singular nouns ending in *-ail* usually take a final *-s* in the plural but there are a few common exceptions.

  o work, job: le travail – les travaux

  o coral: un corail – des coraux

- A few nouns have very irregular plural forms.

  o eye: l'œil *m.* – les yeux

  o sky: le ciel – des cieux (les ciels is also accepted)

Forever Plural

In English, there are nouns that are always plural such as pants, shorts, and scissors. The same is true in French. The table below lists some of the most common nouns that are exclusively plural in French.

condolences	les condoléances f.	lay-kohN-doh-leh-yahNs
contact information	les coordonnées f.	lay-koh-ohr-doh-nay
engagement	les fiançailles f.	lay-fee-yahN-say
expenses	les frais m.	lay-freh
eyeglasses	les lunettes f.	lay-lew-neht
funeral	les funérailles f.	lay-few-nay-rahy
math	les mathématiques f.	lay-mah-tay-mah-teek
neighborhood	les alentours m.	lay-zah-lahN-toor
people	les gens m.	lay-zhahN
scissors	les ciseaux m.	lay-see-zo
trash	les ordures f.	lay-zohr-dewr
vacation	les vacances f.	lay-vah-kahNs

Pesky Nouns

There are some French nouns whose meanings depend on whether they're in the singular or plural form. The following table lists some of the common ones.

Singular	Meaning	Plural	Meaning
le ciseau	chisel	les ciseaux	scissors
le comble	height	les combles	attic

la douceur	sweetness, softness	les douceurs	desserts, sweet talk
l'ouïe *f.*	sense of hearing	les ouïes	gills
la pâte	dough	les pâtes	pasta
la toilette	personal hygiene	les toilettes	restroom
la vacance	vacancy	les vacances	vacation

Exercises

A. Gender

Indicate the gender of the following nouns by using the correct definitive article.

1. atelier

2. ambassade

3. assiette

4. avion

5. chimie

6. café

7. charisme

8. conversation

9. décision

10. été

11. gâteau

12. journal

13. garage

14. maison

15. miracle

16. pomme

17. quittance

18. sortie

19. train

20. université

B. Number

Indicate the plural forms of the following nouns.

1. le table

2. le bras

3. la voix

4. le joujou

5. le seau

6. l'animal

7. le bal

8. le travail

9. le chou

10. le pneu

11. l'œil

12. le livre

13. le val

14. le bâteau

15. le genou

Answers

A. Gender

1. le

2. la

3. la

4. le

5. la

6. le

7. le

8. la

9. la

10. le

11. le

12. le

13. le

14. la

15. le

16. la

17. la

18. le

19. le

20. la

B. Number

1. les tables

2. les bras

3. les voix

4. les joujoux

5. les seaux

6. les animaux

7. les bals

8. les travaux

9. les choux

10. les pneus

11. les yeux

12. les livres

13. les vals

14. les bâteaux

15. les genoux

Chapter 3: Grammar Rules – Verbs and Conjugation

Verbs specify an action or a state of being. Like in English, French verbs change their form depending on who performs the action (subject) and when it's performed (tense) in what is known as conjugation. To conjugate, verbs require a subject noun or pronoun, whether expressed or implied. The table below lists the subject pronouns that you'll need to conjugate verbs.

Person	Singular			Plural		
First	je	*zhuh*	I	nous	*noo*	we
Second	tu	*tew*	you	vous	*voo*	you
Third	il	*eel*	he, it	ils	*eel*	they
	elle	*ehl*	she, it	elles	*ehl*	they
	on	*ohN*	one, we, they			

Notes:

- *Je* is only written in uppercase if used at the beginning of a sentence. It also becomes *j'* when followed by a vowel or a vowel sound.

  o *Oui, j'aime le chocolat.* / Yes, I like chocolate.

- *Tu* is the familiar form of "you" and you can only use it when talking to a friend, relative, child, or pet. Note that you don't drop the *u* when tu is followed by a vowel.

  o *tu arrives* / you arrive

  If you're talking to an older person, someone you're not very familiar with, or a business relation, use the polite form, which is *vous*. Regardless of familiarity, *vous* is always used when you're talking to more than one person.

- *Elles* is only used when the group referred to is composed solely of females. If you're talking about a mixed group, always use *ils* even when it's mostly females.

  o *Elles sont ici.* / They (the nuns) are here.

  o *Ils sont ici.* / They (the priest and the nuns) are here.

- *On* is an indefinite subject pronoun. Although it literally means "one," it's usually used in place of indefinite subjects, such as people, everyone, someone, you, and they. It's also used in informal French to replace *nous* and *vous*.

  o *On dit que ce livre est bon.* / They say this book is good.

  o *On y va!* / Let's go!

Verbs have many forms. When they're not paired with a subject, they exist in their infinitive form. English verbs in their infinitive form are expressed with the word "to": to walk, to eat, to sleep. In French, the infinitive ends in either *-er, -ir,* or *-re.*

Verbs can be grouped into three types depending on their ending. When you conjugate a verb, you change its ending to agree with the subject and the tense. Most of the verbs follow a set pattern of rules depending on the group they belong to and they're known as regular verbs. Verbs that do not adhere to these rules are called irregular verbs.

When you conjugate a verb, you usually drop the ending and what's left is known as the stem. You then add to the stem the ending that corresponds to the subject and tense.

Conjugating regular verbs will be easy once you learn the rules for each group. However, you'll need to memorize the different forms of irregular verbs since they don't follow a pattern.

The Present

The present tense is used to indicate what's happening or how you're feeling. You can also use it to ask for instructions and talk about habits, facts, and what's going to happen in the immediate future.

-er Verbs

It's estimated that 80 to 90% of French verbs end in *-er.* Most of these verbs are also regular. This means that once you learn the pattern of conjugation for *-er* verbs, you can easily conjugate most of the French verbs.

The table that follows shows how regular -er verbs are conjugated in the present tense. Note that even though there are five endings, only the *nous* and *vous* forms are pronounced differently.

Subject	Ending	parler (to speak)	Pronunciation
je	-e	parl**e**	*pahrl*
tu	-es	parl**es**	*pahrl*
il, elle, on	-e	parl**e**	*pahrl*
nous	-ons	parl**ons**	*pahr-lohN*
vous	-ez	parl**ez**	*pahr-lay*
ils, elles	-ent	parl**ent**	*pahrl*

Here are some high-frequency regular -er verbs which you will use quite often.

aider	*eh-day*	to help
aimer	*eh-may*	to like, love
chercher	*shehr-say*	to look for
demander	*duh-mahN-day*	to ask
dépenser	*day-puhN-say*	to spend (money)
donner	*doh-nay*	to give

écouter	*ay-koo-tay*	to listen (to)
étudier	*ay-tew-dyay*	to study
fermer	*fehr-may*	to close
habiter	*ah-bee-tay*	to live (in)
jouer	*zhoo-ay*	to play
oublier	*oo-blee-yay*	to forget
penser	*pahN-say*	to think
préparer	*pray-pah-ray*	to prepare
présenter	*pray-zahN-tay*	to present, introduce
regarder	*ruh-gahr-day*	to look (at), to watch
rencontrer	*rahN-kohN-tray*	to meet
signer	*see-nyay*	to sign
téléphoner	*tay-lay-foh-nay*	to telephone
travailler	*trah-vah-yay*	to work
trouver	*troo-vay*	to find

Irregular Verbs

Changes in irregular *-er* verbs vary from slight change in spelling to a completely different form.

- Verbs ending in *-ger* drop only the final *-r* before adding *-ons* to keep the soft *g* sound.

changer	*shahN-zhay*	changeons	*shahN-zhohN*	we change
manger	*mahN-zhay*	mangeons	*mahN-zhohN*	we eat
nager	*nah-zhay*	nageons	*nah-zhohN*	we swim
voyager	*vwah-yah-zhay*	voyageons	*vwah-yah-zhohN*	we travel

- Verbs ending in *-cer* change the *c* to *ç* before adding *-ons* to keep the soft *s* sound.

annoncer	*ah-nohN-say*	annonçons	*ah-nohN-sohN*	we announce
commencer	*koh-mahN-say*	commençons	*koh-mahN-sohN*	we begin
prononcer	*proh-nohN-say*	prononçons	*proh-nohN-sohN*	we pronounce
remplacer	*rahN-plah-say*	remplaçons	*rahN-plah-sohN*	we replace

- Verbs ending in *-yer* change the *y* to *i* in all but the *nous* and *vous* forms. This change is optional for verbs ending in *-ayer*.

	envoyer (to send)	*ahN-vwah-yay*
je	envoie	*ahN-vwah*
tu	envoies	*ahN-vwah*
il, elle, on	envoie	*ahN-vwah*
nous	envoyons	*ahN-vwah-yohN*
vous	envoyez	*ahN-vwah-yay*
ils, elles	envoient	*ahN-vwah*

Other verbs that follow this pattern are:

- o employer (to use)

- o nettoyer (to clean)

- o payer (to pay [for])

- Verbs that end in *-eler* and *-eter* double the final consonant after dropping *-er* except in the *nous* and *vous* forms. This excludes the verb *acheter* (to buy).

	appeler (to call)	jeter (to throw away)
je	appelle	jette
tu	appelles	jettes
il, elle, on	appelle	jette
nous	appelons	jetons

vous	appelez	jetez
ils, elles	appellent	jettent

Other verbs that follow this pattern are:

- o épeler (to spell out)

- o étenciler (to sparkle)

- o feuilleter (to leaf through a book)

- o renouveler (to renew)

- Verbs ending in *e/é + consonant + er* replace *e/é* with *è* except in the *nous* and *vous* forms.

	acheter (to buy)	préférer (to prefer)
je	achète	préfère
tu	achètes	préfères
il, elle, on	achète	préfère
nous	achetons	préférons
vous	achetez	préférez
ils, elles	achètent	préfèrent

Other verbs that follow this pattern are:

- o amener (to bring)

- o enlever (to take off)

- o espérer (to hope)

- o geler (to freeze)

- o posséder (to own)

- o répéter (to repeat)

- o se lever (to get up)

- o se promener (to take a stroll)

- o suggérer (to suggest)

- *Aller* (to go) is one of the most often used French verbs and it's quite irregular.

	aller (to go)	Pronunciation
je	vais	*veh*
tu	vas	*vah*
il, elle, on	va	*vah*
nous	allons	*ah-lohN*
vous	allez	*ah-lay*
ils, elles	vont	*vohN*

-*ir* Verbs

The table below shows the pattern of conjugation that regular -*ir* verbs follow using the verb *finir*.

Subject	Ending	finir (to finish)	Pronunciation
je	-is	fin**is**	*fee-nee*
tu	-is	fin**is**	*fee-nee*
il, elle, on	-it	fin**it**	*fee-nee*
nous	-issons	fin**issons**	*fee-nee-sohN*
vous	-issez	fin**issez**	*fee-nee-say*
ils, elles	-issent	fin**issent**	*fee-nees*

Here are some common -*ir* verbs that follow this pattern.

choisir	*shwah-seer*	to choose
établir	*ay-tah-bleer*	to establish
grandir	*grahN-deer*	to grow (up)
grossir	*groh-seer*	to gain weight
maigrir	*meh-greer*	to lose weight
mincir	*meen-seer*	to get slimmer

obéir	*oh-bay-eer*	to obey
réagir	*ray-ah-zheer*	to react
réfléchir	*ray-flay-sheer*	to think, reflect
réunir	*ray-ew-neer*	to get together
réussir	*ray-ew-seer*	to succeed
vieillir	*vyay-eer*	to grow old

Irregular -*ir* Verbs

A huge chunk of -*ir* verbs do not follow the pattern of conjugation for regular -*ir* verbs. The good news is that many of them still follow some pattern.

- This group of verbs are conjugated by dropping the stem's final letter in the singular forms before adding the corresponding ending.

Subject	Ending	partir (to leave)	Pronunciation
je	-s	par**s**	*pahr*
tu	-s	par**s**	*pahr*
il, elle, on	-t	par**t**	*pahr*
nous	-ons	part**ons**	*pahr-tohN*
vous	-ez	part**ez**	*pahr-tay*

| ils, elles | -ent | part**ent** | *pahrt* |

Here are some other verbs that follow this pattern.

dormir	*dohr-meer*	to sleep
mentir	*mahN-teer*	to (tell a) lie
sentir	*sahN-teer*	to feel, to smell
servir	*sehr-veer*	to serve
sortir	*sohr-teer*	to go out, to exit

- All verbs that end in *-frir* or *-vrir* and most of those ending in *-llir* follow the pattern of conjugating regular -*er* verbs.

couvrir	*koo-vreer*	to cover
cueillir	*kuh-yeer*	to pick, gather
offrir	*oh-freer*	to offer
ouvrir	*oo-vreer*	to open
souffrir	*soo-freer*	to suffer

- Another sub-group includes the verbs *tenir, venir* and all their derivatives. The table below demonstrates how these verbs are conjugated. Note how the stem changes its spelling in all but the *nous* and *vous* forms. Their endings and the endings of the *partir* group are also the same.

Subject	Ending	tenir (to hold)	venir (to come)
je	-s	tien**s**	vien**s**
tu	-s	tien**s**	vien**s**
il, elle, on	-t	tien**t**	vien**t**
nous	-ons	ten**ons**	ven**ons**
vous	-ez	ten**ez**	ven**ez**
ils, elles	-ent	tienn**ent**	vienn**ent**

Below is a list of common *tenir* and *venir* derivatives.

appartenir	*ah-pahr-tuh-neer*	to belong
contenir	*kohN-tuh-neer*	to contain
détenir	*day-tuh-neer*	to detain
devenir	*duh-vuh-neer*	to become
entretenir	*ahN-truh-tuh-neer*	to maintain, support
maintenir	*maNt-neer*	to maintain
obtenir	*ohb-tuh-neer*	to obtain
prévenir	*pray-vuh-neer*	to prevent
provenir	*proh-vuh-neer*	to come from
retenir	*ruh-tuh-neer*	to retain

revenir	*ruh-vuh-neer*	to come back
soutenir	*soo-tuh-neer*	to support
souvenir	*soo-vuh-neer*	to remember

- Some -*ir* verbs are very irregular and their different conjugated forms are nearly unique. Here are the most common of these verbs.

Subject	avoir (to have)	pouvoir (can)	vouloir (to want)
je	**j'ai**	peux	veux
tu	as	peux	veux
il, elle, on	a	peut	veut
nous	avons	pouvons	voulons
vous	avez	pouvez	voulez
ils, elles	ont	peuvent	veulent

Subject	devoir (must)	voir (to see)
je	dois	vois
tu	dois	vois
il, elle, on	doit	voit
nous	devons	voyons

vous	devez	voyez
ils, elles	doivent	voient

-re Verbs

This group of verbs are sometimes called the -dre verbs. The table below shows how regular verbs in this group are conjugated.

Subject	Ending	perdre (to lose)	Pronunciation
je	-s	perd**s**	*pehr*
tu	-s	perd**s**	*pehr*
il, elle, on	-	perd	*pehr*
nous	-ons	perd**ons**	*pehr-dohN*
vous	-ez	perd**ez**	*pehr-day*
ils, elles	-ent	perd**ent**	*pehrd*

Several dozen verbs in this group are regular. Here are some of the most often used.

attendre	*ah-tahNdr*	to wait (for)
confondre	*kohN-fohNdr*	to confuse
correspondre	*koh-rehs-pohNdr*	to correspond

défendre	*day-fahNdr*	to defend
dépendre	*day-pahNdr*	to depend
descendre	*deh-sahNdr*	to descend
entendre	*ahN-tahNdr*	to understand
fondre	*fohNdr*	to melt
mordre	*mohrdr*	to bite
pendre	*pahNdr*	to hang
perdre	*pehrdr*	to lose
prétendre	*pray-tahNdr*	to claim
rendre	*rahNdr*	to return, give back
répandre	*ray-pahNdr*	to spread
répondre	*ray-pohNdr*	to answer
suspendre	*sew-spahNdr*	to suspend
vendre	*vahNdr*	to sell

Irregular *-re* Verbs

Like *-ir* verbs, majority of *-re* verbs do not follow the pattern of conjugating regular verbs. However, you will notice that the endings used by most of these verbs are the same as the ones used by some irregular *-ir* verbs.

- The stem of verbs ending in *-dire, -fire, -lire,* and *-uire* takes an *s* in the plural forms before adding the appropriate endings.

Subject	Ending	cuire (to cook)	Pronunciation
je	-s	cui**s**	*kwee*
tu	-s	cui**s**	*kwee*
il, elle, on	-t	cui**t**	*kwee*
nous	-ons	cuis**ons**	*kwee-zohN*
vous	-ez	cuis**ez**	*kwee-zay*
ils, elles	-ent	cuis**ent**	*kweez*

Below is a list of commonly used verbs that follow this pattern. However, note that for *dire,* the second person plural form is *dites* and not *disez.*

conduire	*kohN-dweer*	to drive
construire	*kohNs-trweer*	to build
contredire	*kohN-truh-deer*	to contradict
cuire	*kweer*	to cook
détruire	*day-trweer*	to destroy
dire	*deer*	to say, tell

élire	*ay-leer*	to elect
instruire	*ahNs-trweer*	to instruct
introduire	*ahN-troh-dweer*	to introduce
lire	*leer*	to read
nuire	*nweer*	to harm
prédire	*pray-deer*	to predict
réduire	*ray-dweer*	to reduce
reproduire	*reh-proh-dweer*	to reproduce
traduire	*trah-dweer*	to translate

- The stem of verbs ending in *-crire* takes a *v* in the plural form before adding the appropriate endings.

Subject	Ending	écrire (to write)	Pronunciation
je	-s	écri**s**	*ay-kree*
tu	-s	écri**s**	*ay-kree*
il, elle, on	-t	écri**t**	*ay-kree*
nous	-ons	écriv**ons**	*ay-kree-vohN*
vous	-ez	écriv**ez**	*ay-kree-vay*
ils, elles	-ent	écriv**ent**	*ay-kreev*

Commonly used verbs that follow this pattern are listed below.

circonscrire	*seer-kohNs-kreer*	to contain
décrire	*day-kreer*	to describe
prescrire	*prehs-kreer*	to prescribe
proscrire	*prohs-kreer*	to ban
souscrire	*soos-kreer*	to subscribe

o Verbs ending in *-aindre, eindre,* and *-oindre* drop *-dre* in all forms. Their stem also takes a *g* before *n* in the plural form.

Subject	Ending	joindre (to join)	Pronunciation
je	-s	joi**ns**	*zhwa*
tu	-s	joi**ns**	*zhwa*
il, elle, on	-t	joi**nt**	*zhwa*
nous	-ons	joign**ons**	*zhwah-nyohN*
vous	-ez	joign**ez**	*zhway-nyay*
ils, elles	-ent	joign**ent**	*zhwah-nyuh*

Below is a list of commonly used verbs that follow the same pattern.

atteindre	*ah-tahNdr*	to attain
craindre	*krahNdr*	to fear
disjoindre	*dees-zwahNdr*	to disconnect
éteindre	*ay-tahNdr*	to extinguish
peindre	*pahNdr*	to paint
plaindre	*plahNdr*	to feel sorry for
restreindre	*rehs-trahNdr*	to restrict

o Verbs ending in *-ttre* drops a *t* in singular forms and follow the same pattern for conjugating regular *-er* verbs.

Subject	Ending	mettre (to put)	Pronunciation
je	-s	met**s**	*meh*
tu	-s	met**s**	*meh*
il, elle, on	-	met	*meh*
nous	-ons	mett**ons**	*meh-tohN*
vous	-ez	mett**ez**	*meh-tay*
ils, elles	-ent	mett**ent**	*meht*

Below is a list of commonly used verbs that follow the same pattern.

admettre	*ahd-mehtr*	to admit
battre	*bahtr*	to beat
combattre	*kohN-bahtr*	to fight
permettre	*pehr-mehtr*	to permit
promettre	*proh-mehtr*	to promise
soumettre	*soo-mehtr*	to submit

o *Prendre* and all its derivatives also use the same ending as regular -*er* verbs while dropping the *d* in plural forms and taking *n* in the third person plural.

Subject	Ending	prendre (to take)	Pronunciation
je	-s	prend**s**	*prahN*
tu	-s	prend**s**	*prahN*
il, elle, on	-	prend	*prahN*
nous	-ons	pren**ons**	*prah-nohN*
vous	-ez	pren**ez**	*prah-nay*
ils, elles	-ent	prenn**ent**	*prehn*

Commonly used verbs that follow this pattern are listed below.

apprendre	*ah-prahNdr*	to learn
comprendre	*kohN-prahNdr*	to understand
se méprendre	*suh-may-prahNdr*	to be mistaken
reprendre	*reh-prahNdr*	to take again
surprendre	*sewr-prahNdr*	to surprise

- o Verbs ending in *-aître* drop *-tre* in all forms and drop the circumflex except in the third person singular. Their conjugates are shown in the table below.

Subject	apparaître (to appear)	connaître (to know)	disparaître (to disappear)	reconnaître (to recognize)
je	apparais	connais	disparais	reconnais
tu	apparais	connais	disparais	reconnais
il, elle, on	apparaît	connaît	disparaît	reconnaît
nous	apparaissons	connaissons	disparaissons	reconnaissons
vous	apparaissez	connaissez	disparaissez	reconnaissez
ils, elles	apparaissent	connaissent	disparaissent	reconnaissent

- o And finally, here commonly used verbs that have very irregular present tense forms.

	être (to be)	faire (to do)	boire (to drink)
je	suis	fais	bois
tu	es	fais	bois
il, elle, on	est	fait	boit
nous	sommes	faisons	buvons
vous	êtes	faites	buvez
ils, elles	sont	font	boivent

The Past

There are two ways to express actions in the past in French - using the compound past or the imperfect. These two tenses have distinct functions and it's important that you understand how they work so you can express past events accurately.

The Compound Past

The compound past or *passé composé* expresses an event that was started or completed at a certain time in the past. It literally translates to the present perfect in English but in French, it also represents the simple past.

- *J'ai lu le livre.* / I read the book. (simple past)

- *J'ai lu le livre.* / I have read the book. (present perfect)

The compound past is expressed using two verbs – the helping or auxiliary verb and the past participle. The auxiliary verb denotes that an event has occurred. The past participle expresses the actual event that occurred.

The Past Participle

The past participle is quite easy to learn since there's only one form for each verb. For regular verbs, drop the *-er*, *-ir*, or *-re* and add the appropriate ending as illustrated below.

-er verbs	*-ir* verbs	*-re* verbs
danser (to dance)	finir (to finish)	entendre (to understand)
dans**é**	fin**i**	entend**u**

All *-er* verbs behave as regular verbs in the past participle. Most of the irregular *-ir* and *-re* in the present tense also have irregular past participle. The table below lists the most common irregular verbs and their past participle forms.

acquérir	acquis	acquired
apprendre	appris	learned
asseoir	assis	sat
avoir	eu	had
boire	bu	drank, drunk
comprendre	compris	understood
conduire	conduit	drove, driven
connaître	connu	known

construire	construit	built
courir	couru	ran, run
couvrir	couvert	covered
croire	cru	believed
découvrir	découvert	discovered
devoir	dû	had to
dire	dit	said, told
écrire	écrit	wrote, written
être	été	was, been
faire	fait	done, did, made
falloir	fallu	had to
joindre	joint	joined
lire	lu	read
mettre	mis	put
mourir	mort	died
naitre	né	was born
offrir	offert	offered
ouvrir	ouvert	opened
peindre	peint	painted

permettre	permis	allowed
pleuvoir	plu	rained
prendre	pris	took
produire	produit	produced
pouvoir	pu	was able to
recevoir	reçu	received
rire	ri	laughed
savoir	su	knew
suivre	suivi	followed
tenir	tenu	held
vivre	vécu	lived
voir	vu	saw, seen
vouloir	voulu	wanted

The Auxiliary Verb

Avoir and *être* conjugated in their present tense are used as auxiliary verbs in the compound past tense. Below is a table showing the conjugated forms of these helping verbs for reference.

Subject	avoir (to have)	être (to be)
je	**j'ai**	suis

tu	as	es
il, elle, on	a	est
nous	avons	sommes
vous	avez	êtes
ils, elles	ont	sont

In most cases, *avoir* is used as the helping verb. However, there are a few common verbs that use *être* to form the compound past.

aller	allé	went
arriver	arrivé	arrived
descendre	descendu	went down
devenir	devenu	became
entrer	entré	entered
monter	monté	went up
mourir	mort	died
naître	né	was born
passer	passé	passed by
partir	parti	left
rentrer	rentré	returned
rester	resté	remained

retourner	retourné	returned
revenir	revenu	returned
sortir	sorti	went out, exited
tomber	tombé	fell, fallen
venir	venu	came

Whenever *être* is used, the past participle must agree in gender and number with the subject.

Masculine Subjects	Feminine Subjects	English
Je suis parti.	Je suis parti**e**.	I left.
Tu es parti.	Tu es parti**e**.	You left.
Vous êtes parti.	Vous êtes parti**e**.	You left. (singular, formal)
Il est parti.	Elle est parti**e**.	He/she left.
Nous sommes parti**s**.	Nous sommes parti**es**.	We left.
Vous êtes parti**s**.	Vous êtes parti**es**.	You left. (plural)
Ils sont parti**s**.	Elles sont parti**es**.	They left.

Whenever *avoir* is used, the past participle remains unchanged.

o *Il a mangé des mangues.* / He ate mangoes.

- *Elle a mangé des mangues.* / She ate mangoes.

- *Nous avons mangé des mangues.* / We ate mangoes.

Using the Compound Past

The compound past is used in the following instances:

- Describing an event that was started completed in the past

  - *Le film a commencé à huit heures.* / The movie started at eight.

  - *Nous sommes rentrés hier.* / We returned yesterday.

- Describing an action that was repeated a specific number of times

  - *J'ai lu le livre deux fois.* / I read the book twice.

The Imperfect

The imperfect or *imparfait* indicates repeated or incomplete events or ongoing state of being in the past. In English, it usually translates to was/were + *-ing* form of verb.

To conjugate the imperfect, take the *nous* form of the verb in the present tense. Drop the *-ons* ending and add the appropriate ending. The table below shows the imperfect endings and a few conjugated examples.

Subject	Ending	parler	finir	perdre	être
je	-ais	parlais	finissais	perdais	étais

tu	-ais	parlais	finissais	perdais	étais
il, elle, on	-ait	parlait	finissait	perdait	était
nous	-ions	parlions	finissions	perdions	étions
vous	-iez	parliez	finissiez	perdiez	étiez
ils, elles	-aient	parlaient	finissaient	perdaient	étaient

Note that because the *nous* form of *être* (sommes) doesn't end in *-ons*, it uses *ét-* as stem.

Using the Imperfect

The imperfect is used in the following instances:

- Describing what was happening or what used to happen repeatedly in the past.

  - *Je travaillais toute la journée.* / I was working all day.

  - *Elle visitait tous le dimanches.* / She used to visit every Sunday.

- Expressing a state of mind with verbs such as *croire, penser, pouvoir, savoir,* and *vouloir*

  - *Je savais ce que tu voulais.* / I knew what you wanted.

- Describing feelings, age, weather, and time

  - *J'étais très fatigué.* / I was very tired.

- *Nous étions quinze quand nous nous sommes rencontrés.* / We were 15 when we met.

- *C'était le matin et il faisait nuageux.* / It was morning and it was cloudy. /

- Describing an ongoing situation when another event occurred

  - *Tu dormais quand je suis revenu.* / You were sleeping when I returned.

The Future

In French, actions or states that are yet to occur can be expressed in three ways – through the simple future tense, the near future tense, or the present tense.

The Simple Future

The simple future is the equivalent of the English "will" + infinitive. The word "will" has no French translation and a regular -*er* or -*ir* verb conjugated in the simple future is the entire verb combined with the appropriate ending. For regular -*re* verbs, the final *e* is dropped before adding the ending.

Subject	Ending	manger (to eat)	vendre (to sell)
je	-ai	manger**ai**	vendr**ai**
tu	-as	manger**as**	vendr**as**
il, elle, on	-a	manger**a**	vendr**a**
nous	-ons	manger**ons**	vendr**ons**

| vous | -ez | manger**ez** | vendr**ez** |
| ils, elles | -ont | manger**ont** | vendr**ont** |

- ○ *Je <u>mangerai</u> plus tard.* / I will eat later.

- ○ *Nous <u>vendrons</u> la maison.* / We will sell the house.

Irregular Verbs

Irregular verbs in the simple future tense use the same endings as regular verbs but they do not use the infinitive as stem or the infinitive undergoes some spelling changes.

- Verbs ending in *-yer* (except *envoyer*) change their *y* to *i*

- Some verbs change *e to è*

acheter	achèter-	to buy
achever	achèver-	to complete
amener	amèner-	to cause
lever	lèver	to lift
promener	promèner	to take for a walk

- Some verbs double the consonant before *-er*

appeler	appeller-	to call
épeler	épeller-	to spell
feuilleter	feuilletter-	to leaf through a book

jeter	jetter-	to throw away
projeter	projetter-	to plan
rappeler	rappeller-	to recall
rejeter	rejetter-	to reject
renouveler	renouveller-	to renew

- Majority of irregular verbs drop their infinitive ending and undergo spelling change

acquérir	acquerr-	to acquire
aller	ir-	to go
avoir	aur-	to have
courir	courr-	to run
devoir	devr-	to have to
discourir	discourr-	to elaborate
envoyer	enverr-	to send
être	ser-	to be
faire	fer-	to do
falloir	faudr-	to be necessary
maintenir	maintiendr-	to maintain
mourir	mourr-	to die

pleuvoir	pleuvr-	to rain
pouvoir	pourr-	to be able to
recevoir	recevr-	to receive
savoir	saur-	to know
tenir	tiendr-	to hold
valoir	vaudr-	to be worth
venir	viendr-	to come
voir	verr-	to see
vouloir	voudr-	to want

The Near Future

The near future tense is used to indicate an action or state that will happen in the very near future. It is formed by combining the present tense form of *aller* and the infinitive or the verb. This is the equivalent of the English "going to" + infinitive.

- o *Je vais manger une pomme.* / I'm going to eat an apple.

- o *Nous allons vendre la maison.* / We're going to sell the house.

The Present as Future

In spoken French, the future can be expressed using the present tense of the verb and an expression that implies the future.

- o *Je mange bientôt.* / I'm going to eat soon.

o *Nous <u>vendons</u> la maison le mois prochain.* / We will sell the house next month.

Below is a list of time expressions indicating the future.

Expression	English
après	after
bientôt	soon
ensuite / puis	then/next
plus tard	later
ce soir	tonight / this evening
cet après-midi	this afternoon
demain	tomorrow
demain matin	tomorrow morning
demain après midi	tomorrow afternoon
demain soir	tomorrow night / evening
après-demain	the day after tomorrow
[day of the week] + prochain	next + [day of the week]
la semaine prochaine	next week
le mois prochain	next month
le weekend prochain	next weekend
l'année prochaine	next year
un jour	one day

Mood of the Verb

Aside from tenses, verbs also have different moods. While the former refers to when an action is performed, the latter describes the attitude of the speaker toward the state or action of the verb.

The indicative is the most often used mood of the verb. You use it when you make a statement or ask a question. Other moods of the verb are imperative, subjunctive, and conditional.

The Present Subjunctive

The subjunctive expresses emotion, doubt, uncertainty, wishing, or wanting. It's used in sentences with two clauses joined by *que* and with different subjects.

- *Je doute qu'il puisse le faire.* / I doubt that he can do it.

- *Je souhaite que nous puissions voyager à tout moment.* / I wish we can travel anytime.

The present subjunctive of a regular verb is formed by dropping the final *-ent* of the third person plural in the present tense before adding the appropriate ending.

Subject	Ending	parler (to speak)
je	-e	parle
tu	-es	parles
il, elle, on	-e	parle
nous	-ions	parlions

vous	-iez	parl**iez**
ils, elles	-ent	parl**ent**

- The following verbs have irregular stems in the subjunctive.

  - *faire: fass-* (to make)

  - *pouvoir: puiss-* (to be able to)

  - *savoir: sach-* (to know)

- These verbs have two different stems in the subjunctive.

Subject	je, tu, il, ils	nous, vous
boire (to drink)	boive-	buv-
prendre (to take)	prenne-	pren-
envoyer (to send)	envoi-	envoy-
acheter (to buy)	achèt-	achet-
appeler (to call)	appell-	appel-
jeter (to throw)	jett-	jet-
répéter (to repeat)	répèt	répét-
aller (to go)	aill-	all-
vouloir (to want)	veuill-	voul-

- *Avoir* and *être* are quite irregular in the subjunctive. These are their different conjugated forms.

Subject	avoir (to have)	être (to be)
je	aie	sois
tu	aies	sois
il, elle, on	ait	soit
nous	ayons	soyons
vous	ayez	soyez
ils, elles	aient	soient

The Conditional

This mood expresses actions or events whose occurrence depend on certain conditions. In English, the conditional is a combination of the modal verb would and the infinitive. The French conditional is formed by adding the endings listed below to the future stem of all verbs.

Subject	Ending	aller/ir- (to speak)
je	-ais	ir**ais**
tu	-ais	ir**ais**
il, elle, on	-ait	ir**ait**
nous	-ions	ir**ions**
vous	-iez	ir**iez**
ils, elles	-aient	ir**aient**

The conditional is primarily used in if-then sentence constructions although then is not translated in French. The then clause uses the conditional form of the verb while the *si* (if) clause contains verbs in the present or past tense.

- o *Il nous rejoindrait si on l'invitait.* / He would join us if we invited him.

- o *Ils seraient là s'il ne pleut pas.* / They'd be here if it doens't rain.

The conditional form of *vouloir* (to want) is used to express a polite request

- • *Je voudrais du café.* / I'd like some coffee.

Exercises

Complete the following sentences with the correct conjugated verb.

A. The Present

1. *Je (parler) à mon chien.* / I talk to my dog.

2. *Nous (étudier) le français.* / We're studying French.

3. *Elle (penser) toujours à toi.* / She always thinks of you.

4. *Ce magasin (vendre) des vêtements.* / That store sells clothes.

5. *Nous (voyager) souvent.* / We travel often.

6. *Le garçon (aller) à l'école.* / The boy is going to school.

7. *Tu (avoir) mes clés.* / You (singular) have my keys.

8. *Mon animal de compagnie (vouloir) plus de nourriture.* / My pet wants more food.

9. *Nous (peindre) le mur.* / We are painting the wall.

10. *Les (être) ici.* / They're here.

B. The Past

1. *Elle (oublier) son parapluie.* / She forgot her umbrella.

2. *Il (écrire) des poèmes le week-end.* / He used to write poems on weekends.

3. *J' (recevoir) un cadeau.* / I received a gift.

4. *Il (devenir) médecin.* / He became a doctor.

5. *Ils (danser).* / They were dancing.

6. *Nous (parler) toute la nuit.* / We talked all night.

7. *Je (penser) que tu (dormir).* / I thought you were sleeping.

8. *Ils (aller) en France.* / They went to France.

9. *Elle (vouloir) gagner.* / She wanted to win.

10. *Je (manger) quand tu (arriver).* / I was eating when you arrived.

C. The Future

1. *Nous (acheter) une nouvelle robe.* / We're going to buy a new dress.

2. *Votre plante (mourir).* / Your plant is going to die.

3. *Votre professeur (appeler) ton nom.* / Your teacher will call your name.

4. *Je (jeter) tous ses vêtements.* / I will throw away all his clothes.

5. *Je (renouveler) mon permis.* / I'm going to renew my license.

6. *Il (pleuvoir) cet après-midi.* / It's going to rain this afternoon.

7. *Vous (recevoir) un email.* / You will receive an e-mail.

8. *Ils (venir) ici la semaine prochaine.* / They will come here next week.

9. *Tu (être) un bon père.* / You will be a good father.

10. *Je le (faire) la semaine prochaine.* / I'll do it next week.

Answers

A.

1. parle

2. étudions

3. pense

4. vend

5. voyageons

6. va

7. as

8. veut

9. peignons

10. sont

B.

1. a oublié

2. écrivait

3. ai reçu

4. est devenu

5. dansaient

6. avons parlé

7. pensais, dormais

8. sont allés

9. voulait

10. mangeais, es arrivé

C.

1. allons acheter

2. va mourir

3. appellera

4. vais jeter

5. vais renouveler

6. va pleuvoir

7. recevrez

8. viendront

9. seras

10. ferai

Chapter 4: Grammar Rules – Adjectives and Adverbs

Adjectives

In both English and French, adjectives have the same purpose - they describe nouns and pronouns. While English adjectives only have one form, French adjectives can have up to four. That's because French adjectives must agree with the gender and number of the word they modify.

Gender

The default form of adjectives in French is masculine singular. In most cases, adding a final *e* makes it feminine. Below is a list of some common adjectives in masculine and feminine forms. Note that the addition of letter usually changes the adjective's pronunciation.

Masculine	Pronunciation	Feminine	Pronunciation	Meaning
âgé	*ah-zhay*	âgée	*ah-zhay*	old
américain	*ah-may-ree-kahN*	américaine	*ah-may-ree-kehn*	American
amusant	*ah-mew-zahN*	amusante	*ah-mew-zahNt*	amusing
blond	*blohN*	blonde	*blohNd*	blond
charmant	*shahr-*	charmant	*shahr-*	charming

	mahN	e	*mahNt*	
chaud	*sho*	chaude	*shod*	hot, warm
élégant	*ay-lay-gahN*	élégante	*ay-lay-gahNt*	elegant
fort	*fohr*	forte	*fohrt*	strong
français	*frahN-seh*	français	*frahN-sehz*	French
grand	*grahN*	grande	*grahNd*	big
joli	*zhoh-lee*	jolie	*zhoh-lee*	pretty
lourd	*loor*	lourde	*loohrd*	heavy
noir	*nwahr*	noire	*nwahr*	black
occupé	*oh-kew-pay*	occupée	*oh-kew-pay*	busy
petit	*puh-tee*	petite	*puh-teet*	small
poli	*poh-lee*	polie	*poh-lee*	polite
surpris	*sewr-pree*	surprise	*sewr-preez*	surprised
vert	*vehr*	verte	*vehrt*	green

When an adjective ends in *-e*, there's no need to add a final *-e* to get the femine form. The pronunciation also stays the same.

Masculine / Feminine	Pronunciation	Meaning
aimable	*ah-mahbl*	kind, pleasant
célèbre	*say-lehbr*	famous
comique	*koh-meek*	comical
drôle	*drol*	funny
facile	*fah-seel*	easy
faible	*fahbl*	weak
honnête	*oh-neht*	honest
malade	*mah-lahd*	sick
mince	*maNs*	thin
pauvre	*povr*	poor
propre	*prohpr*	clean
sale	*sahl*	dirty
symphatique	*seem-fa-teek*	nice
triste	*treest*	sad
vide	*veed*	empty

Irregular Adjectives

A number of adjectives undergo spelling change to form the feminine.

- When a singular masculine adjective ends in -*eux,* the feminine is formed by replacing -*x* with -*se.* This change gives the feminine form final *z* sound.

Masculine	Pronunciation	Feminine	Pronunciation	Meaning
affectueux	*ah-fehk-tew-uh*	affectueuse	*ah-fehk-tew-uhz*	affectionate
ambitieux	*ahN-bee-syuh*	ambitieuse	*ahN-bee-syuhz*	ambitious
chanceux	*shahN-suh*	chanceuse	*shahN-suhz*	lucky
curieux	*kew-ryuh*	curieuse	*kew-ryuhz*	curious
dangereux	*dahN-zhuh-ruh*	dangereuse	*dahN-zhuh-ruhz*	dangerous
délicieux	*day-lee-syuh*	délicieuse	*day-lee-syuhz*	delicious
généreux	*zhay-nay-ruh*	généreuse	*zhay-nay-ruhz*	generous
heurex	*uh-ruh*	heureuse	*uh-ruhz*	happy
paresseux	*pahr-suh*	paresseuse	*pahr-suhz*	lazy

| sérieux | *say-ryuh* | sérieuse | *say-ryuhz* | serious |

- Adjectives ending in *f* change *f* to *ve* to form the feminine.

Masculine	Pronunciation	Feminine	Pronunciation	Meaning
actif	*ahk-teef*	active	*ahk-teev*	active
attentif	*ah-tahN-teef*	attentive	*ah-tahN-teev*	attentive
imaginatif	*ee-mah-zhee-nah-teef*	imaginative	*ee-mah-zhee-nah-teev*	imaginative
impulsif	*aN-pewl-seef*	impulsive	*aN-pewl-seef*	impulsive
naïf	*nah-eef*	naive	*nah-eev*	naive
neuf	*nuhf*	neuve	*nuhv*	new
sportif	*spohr-teef*	sportive	*spohr-teev*	athletic

- Adjectives ending in *-er* form the feminine by changing *-er* to *-ère*.

Masculine	Pronunciation	Feminine	Pronunciation	Meaning
cher	*shehr*	chère	*shehr*	dear, expensive

dernier	*dehr-nyay*	dernière	*dehr-nyehr*	last
entier	*ahN-tyay*	entière	*ahN-tyehr*	entire
étranger	*ay-trahN-zhay*	étrangère	*ay-trahN-zhehr*	foreign
fier	*fyehr*	fière	*fyehr*	proud
léger	*lay-gay*	légère	*lay-gehr*	light
premier	*pruh-myay*	première	*pruh-myehr*	first

- Some adjectives double their final consonant and add *-e* to form the fiminine.

Masculine	Pronunciation	Feminine	Pronunciation	Meaning
ancien	*ahN-syaN*	ancienne	*ahN-syehn*	ancient
bas	*bah*	basse	*bahs*	low
bon	*bohN*	bonne	*bohn*	good
européen	*ew-roh-pay-aN*	européenne	*ew-roh-pay-ehn*	European
gentil	*zhahN-tee-y*	gentille	*zhahN-tee-y*	nice, kind
gros	*gro*	grosse	*gros*	fat, big
mignon	*mee-nyohN*	mignonne	*mee-nyohN*	cute

- Some adjectives are quite irregular and don't follow any rules.

Masculine	Pronunciation	Feminine	Pronunciation	Meaning
beau*	*bo*	belle	*behl*	beautiful
blanc	*blahN*	blanche	*blahNsh*	white
complet	*kohN-pleh*	complète	*kohN-pleht*	complete
doux	*doo*	douce	*doos*	sweet, gentle
faux	*fo*	fausse	*fos*	false
favori	*fah-voh-ree*	favorite	*fah-voh-reet*	favorite
frais	*freh*	fraîche	*frehsh*	fresh
franc	*frahN*	franche	*frahNsh*	frank
long	*lohN*	longue	*lohNg*	long
nouveau*	*noo-vo*	nouvelle	*noo-vehl*	new
public	*pew-bleek*	publique	*pew-bleek*	public
sec	*suhk*	séche	*saysh*	dry
secret	*seh-kreh*	secréte	*seh-krayt*	secret
vieux*	*vyuh*	vieille	*vyay*	old

- These adjectives have special forms which are used when followed by a noun that starts with a vowel or vowel sound.

  - beau: un bel appartement / a beautiful apartment

  - nouveau: un nouvel atelier / a new studio

  - vieux: un vel avion / an old airplane

Number

Making adjectives plural is quite simple. You simply add an -s to the masculine or feminine form. For most adjectives ending in -eau, you have to add -x. If the singular adjective already ends in -s or -x, there's no need to do anything.

  - chaud – chauds

  - gentille – gentilles

  - surpris – surpris

  - vieux – vieux

  - nouveau – nouveaux

Note that adding and -s or -x doesn't change the adjective's pronunciation, unless it's followed by a word that begins with a vowel or vowel sound.

For adjectives ending in -al, the plural is usually formed by changing -al to -aux. This changes the words pronunciation.

  - principal – principaux

  - spécial – spéciaux

Placement

French adjectives are commonly placed after the noun they modify. This is quite the opposite with English.

- o une robe <u>bleu</u> / a blue robe

- o un homme <u>intéressant</u> / an interesting man

Some adjectives always precede the noun they modify. Below is a table listing the most commonly used of these adjectives.

beau	une belle histoire	a beautiful story
bon	un bon chien	a good dog
court	une courte distance	a short distance
grand	la grande maison	the big house
gros	le gros arbre	the large tree
jeune	un jeune couple	a young couple
joli	un joli visage	a pretty face
long	une longue corde	a long roap
mauvais	un mauvais rêve	a bad dream
petit	les petites boîtes	the small boxes
vieux	une vieille voiture	an old car
autre	l'autre côté	the other side
chaque	chaque étudiant	each student

dernier	le dernier morceau	the last piece
plusieurs	plusieurs idées	several ideas
quelques	quelques jours	a few days
tel	une telle aventure	such an adventure
tout*	tous les pays	all countries

Note: *Tout* always precedes both noun and definite articles.

If you're using more than one adjective, put each adjective according to whether it should come before or after the noun. Use the word *et* (and) between adjectives in the same position.

- o *un vieil appartement sale* – a dirty old apartment

- o *un homme charmant et intelligent* – a charming and intelligent man

Pesky Adjectives

Some adjectives can be placed before or after the noun they modify. Their meanings change according to their location. Usually, the meaning is more figurative when the adjective precedes the noun.

Adjective	Before the Noun	After the Noun
ancient	former	antique, old
certain	some	sure

cher	dear	expensive
dernier	final	previous/last (time expression)
grand (people)	great	tall
pauvre	wretched, miserable	poor, broke
propre	own	clean
seul	only	alone
simple	mere	simple

- ○ *mon <u>cher</u> ami* / my dear friend

- ○ *un bijou <u>cher</u>* / an expensive jewelry

Adverbs

Adverbs are words or expressions that describe verbs, adjectives, and sometimes, other adverbs. Unlike adjectives, they don't have masculine, feminine, or plural forms.

Types of Adverbs

Most adverbs can be categorized depending on the type of information they provide or what question they answer.

Adverbs of Manner

This group of adverbs describe how an action is done and answers the question *comment* (how). Most of them end in -

ment which most of the time, correspond to English adverbs that end in *-ly*. Adverbs of manner are usually formed from singular feminine adjectives and singular masculine adjectives ending in a vowel.

Adjective	Adverb	Pronunciation	Meaning
absolu	absolument	*ahb-soh-lew-mahN*	absolutely
active	activement	*ahk-teev-mahN*	actively
complete	completement	*kohN-pleht-mahN*	completely
continuelle	continuellement	*kohN-tee-new-ehl-mahN*	continuously
douce	doucement	*doos-mahN*	gently
éventuelle	éventuellement	*ay-vahN-tew-ehl-mahN*	possibly
fière	fièrement	*fyehr-mahN*	proudly
heureuse	heureusement	*uh-ruhz-mahN*	fortunately
lente	lentement	*lahNt-mahN*	slowly
nécessaire	nécessairem	*nay-seh-*	necessarily

	ent	*sehr-mahN*	
normale	normalemen t	*nohr-mahl-mahN*	normally
passionné	passionném ent	*pah-syoh-nay-mahN*	enthusiastic ally
poli	poliment	*poh-lee-mahN*	politely
rapide	rapidement	*rah-peed-mahN*	quickly
sérieuse	sérieusemen t	*say-ree-uhz-mahN*	seriously
seule	seulement	*suhl-mahN*	only
vrai	vraiment	*vreh-mahN*	truly, really

Exceptions:

- o *bref – brièvement* (briefly)

- o *gentil – gentiment* (kindly)

- There are a few common adverbs that require an accute accent on the vowel before *-ment.*

commune	communément	*koh-mew-nay-mahN*	commonly
conforme	conformément	*kohN-fohr-may-mahN*	in accordance

intense	intensément	*aN-tahN-say-mahN*	intensely
précis	précisément	*pray-see-say-mahN*	precisely

- Adjectives that end in -*ant* or -*ent* drop their ending and add -*amment* or –*emment*.

apparent	apparemment	*ah-pah-reh-mahN*	apparently
bruyant	bruyamment	*brew-yah-mahN*	loudly
constant	constamment	*kohN-stah-mahN*	constantly
courant	couramment	*koo-rah-mahN*	fluently
évident	évidemment	*ay-vee-deh-mahN*	evidently
patient	patiemment	*pah-syeh-mahN*	patiently
prudent	prudemment	*prew-deh-mahN*	prudently
recent	récemment	*ray-seh-mahN*	recently

Exception: *lent – lentement* (slowly)

- Some adverbs of manner are not derived from adjectives and don't end in *-ment.*

ainsi	*aN-see*	thus
bien	*byaN*	well
debout	*duh-boo*	standing up
exprès	*ehks-preh*	on purpose
mal	*mahl*	badly, poorly
mieux	*myuh*	better
pire	*peer*	worse
vite	*veet*	quickly
volontiers	*voh-lohN-tyay*	willingly

- A few adjectives do not take any ending when used in certain expressions. The meaning of the adjective slightly changes and since it functions as an adverb, it doesn't have to agree in gender and number.

Adjective	Adverb	English
bas (low)	parler bas	to speak softly
bon (good)	sentir bon	to smell good
cher (expensive)	coùter cher	to cost a lot
clair (clear)	voir clair	to see clearly

dur (hard)	travailler dur	to work hard
fort (strong)	parler fort	to speak loud
mauvais (bad)	sentir mauvais	to smell bad

Adverbs of Frequency

This group of adverbs describe how often an action occurs.

Adverb	Pronunciation	English
d'habitude	*dah-bee-tewd*	usually
encore	*ahN-kohr*	again
jamais	*zhah-meh*	never, ever
parfois	*pahr-fwah*	sometimes, occasionally
quelquefois	*kehl-kuh-fwah*	sometimes
rarement	*rahr-mahN*	rarely
souvent	*soo-vahN*	often
toujours	*too-zhoor*	always, still

Adverbs of Place

This group of adverbs answer the question *où* (where).

Adverb	Pronunciation	English
à l'interieur	*ah*	inside
dehors	*duh-ohr*	outside
à côté	*ah-ko-tay*	next door, next to
à droite	*ah-drawht*	to the right
à gauche	*ah gosh*	to the left
devant	*duh-vahN*	in front
derrière	*dehr-ryehr*	behind
où	*oo*	where
ici	*ee-see*	here
là	*lah*	there
là-bas	*lah-bah*	over there
là-dedans	*lah-duh-dahN*	in here, in there
loin (de)	*lawn (duh)*	far
près (de)	*preh (duh)*	close, nearby
partout	*pahr-too*	everywhere
quelque part	*kehl-kuh-pahr*	somewhere

nulle part	*newl-pahr*	nowhere
en haut	*ahN-o*	up, upstairs
en bas	*ahN-ba*	down, downstairs
dessus	*deh-sew*	on top of
au fond	*o-fohN*	at the bottom
sous	*soo*	under

Many adverbs of place (including some in the table above) also operate as prepositions. The difference is that when used as prepositions, they require an object. Without and object, they are considered adverbs. In addition, a phrase consisting of a preposition and its object – also called a prepositional phrase – is an adverb.

- Adverb: *La balle est tombée <u>dehors</u>.* / The ball fell outside.

- Preposition: *La balle est tombée <u>en dehors</u> de la boîte.* / The ball fell outside the box.

- Prepositional phrase/adverb: *en dehors de la boîte* / outside the box

Adverbs of Quantity

These group of adverbs answer the question *combien* (how many/how much).

Adverb	Pronunciation	English
assez (de)	*ah-say(-duh)*	enough, quite, fairly
autant	*o-tahN*	as much, as many
beaucoup	*bo-koo*	a lot
combien	*kohN-byaN*	how many, much
davantage	*dah-vahN-tazh*	more
encore de	*ahN-kohr-duh*	more
environ	*ahN-vee-rohN*	approximately, around
moins	*mwaN*	less, fewer
pas mal	*pah-mahl*	quite a few
(un) peu (de)	*(uhN-)puh(-duh)*	little, few, not very
plus	*plew*	more
presque	*prehsk*	almost
seulement	*suhl-mahN*	only
si	*see*	so
tant	*tahN*	so much, so many
tellement	*tehl-mahN*	so much

très	*treh*	very
trop	*tro*	too much, too many

Adverbs of Time

This group of adverbs answers the question *quand* (when).

Adverb	Pronunciation	English
actuellement	*ahk-tew-ehl-mahN*	currently
alors	*ah-lohr*	then
après	*ah-preh*	after
aujourd'hui	*oh-zhoor-dwee*	today
avant	*ah-vahN*	before
bientôt	*byaN-to*	soon
d'abord	*dah-bohr*	first, at first
déjà	*day-zhah*	already
demain	*duh-maN*	tomorrow
depuis	*duh-pwee*	since
enfin	*ahN-faN*	finally, at last
ensuite	*ahN-sweet*	then, next
hier	*yehr*	yesterday

immédiatement	*ee-may-dyaht-mahN*	immediately
jamais	*zhah-meh*	never, ever
longtemps	*lohN-tahN*	a long time
maintenant	*maNt-nahN*	now
précédemment	*pray-say-deh-mahN*	previously
puis	*pwee*	then
plus tard	*plew tahr*	later
récemment	*ray-seh-mahN*	recently
tard	*tahr*	late
tôt	*to*	early
tout de suite	*toot sweet*	immediately, right away

Placement

In general, adverbs are placed after the word they modify. However, their position still depends on the type of the word or words they modify.

Adverbs modifying a verb are usually placed after the conjugated verb. Note that in the compound past, both verbs are conjugated so the adverb is placed after the second verb. In the near-future tense, the second verb is in the infinitive form so the adverb is placed after the conjugated form of *aller*.

- *Nous apprécions <u>vraimant</u> cela.* / We really appreciate it.

- *Il marchait <u>lentement</u>.* / He walked slowly.

- *Je me suis couché <u>tot</u>.* / I went to bed early.

- *Elle va <u>évidemment</u> gagner.* / She's obviously going to win.

In the compound past tense, some very common adverbs are placed between the auxilliary verb and the past participle. These adverbs are *bien, beaucoup, déjà, mal, probablement, tellement, toujours, vite,* and *vraiment*.

- *J'ai <u>déjà</u> mangé.* / I already ate.

- *Nous l'avons <u>vraiment</u> fait.* / We really did it.

When an adverb modifies and adjective or another adverb, it is placed before the word it modifies.

- *C'est <u>très</u> beau.* / It's very beautiful.

- *Mon chien ronfle <u>assez</u> souvent.* / My dog snores quite often.

Adverbs of time are usually placed at the end of a sentence.

- *Nous serons là <u>bientôt</u>.* / We will be there soon.

- *Il est parti <u>hier</u>.* / He left yesterday.

French adverbs can never be placed right after the subject.

- *Il l'aime <u>évidemment</u>.* / He obviously likes her.

- *Je vais parfois au cinéma.* / I sometimes go to the movies.

Making Comparisons

French adjectives and adverbs have comparative and superlative forms. They are used to compare the elements they modify and provide a more detailed description. To make comparisons, comparative and superlative adverbs are used.

The Comparative

Comparative adverbs are used to compare two elements. There are three types of comparisons – superiority, inferiority, and equality. The comparison can either be stated or implied.

superiority	plus (que)	more (than)
inferiority	moins (que)	less (than)
equality	aussi (as)	as (as)

The first word is required and is always followed by the adjective or adverb. The word *que* (than) is followed by the element compared against. *Que* is not used when the comparison is implied.

- *Elle est plus grande que lui.* / She is taller than him.

- *Mon histoire est moins excitante.* / My story is less exciting.

- *Elle travaille aussi dur que les autres.* / She works as hard as the others.

Note that just like in English, you can't say *plus bon* (more good). In French, the word for better is *meilleur*. Since it's an adjective, it has to agree with the gender and number of the noun it modifies.

- o *Mon chien est meilleur que ton chat.* / My dog is better than your cat.

- o *Leurs produits sont meilleurs.* / Their products are better.

When comparing quantity of nouns, *autant* is used instead of *aussi*. The noun or nouns being compared are also preceded by *de* (of).

- o *J'ai plus d'expérience que toi.* / I have more experience than you.

- o *Elle a moins d'amis que d'ennemis.* / She has fewer friends than enemies.

- o *Il y a autant de bananes que de pommes.* / There are as many bananas as apples.

When comparing verbs, the comparative adverb is placed after the verb.

- o *Je mange plus que toi.* / I eat more than you do.

- o *Il dort moins que nous.* / He sleeps less than us.

- o *Ils voyagent autant qu'ils le peuvant.* / They travel as much as they can.

Some adjectives already indicate comparison so they don't need the words *plus, moins,* and *aussi* when making comparison. With these adjectives, *à* or *de* is used instead of *que* to introduce the second element of comparison.

- *différent de* – different from

- *identique à* – identical to

- *inférieur à* – inferior to

- *pareil à* – same as

- *semblable à* – similar to

- *supérieur à* – superior to

The Superlative

To indicate that something is the most or the least, superlative adverbs are used. These adverbs are *le plus* and *le moins*.

When comparing adjectives, the article must agree with the gender and number of their noun. The superlative adverb always precedes the adjective it modifies. When this adjective is supposed to come after the noun, the superlative does the same.

- *Elle est l'étudiante la plus âgée de sa classe.* / She's the oldest student in her class.

- *Ce sont les athlètes les plus forts.* / They're the stongest athletes.

Note: The superlative forms of *bon* and *mauvais* are *le meilleur* and *le pire.*

When the adjective is supposed to precede the noun, the superlative can follow or precede it. Both constructions are correct but placing the superlative after the noun makes your statement stronger.

- o *J'ai acheté la plus petite boîte.* / I bought the smallest box.

- o *J'ai acheté la boîte la plus petite.* / I bought the smallest box.

The same superlatives are used when comparing adverbs and verbs. The difference is that there's no need for the articles to agree in gender and number. The superlative also goes right after the verb.

- o *Je cours le plus lentement.* / I run the slowest.

- o *Il travaille le moins efficacement.* / He works the least effectively.

Note: The superlative form of *bien* is *le mieux*.

When referring to quantity of nouns, the superlative adverbs should always be followed by *de*.

- o *J'ai fait le plus d'argent.* / I made the most money.

- o *Notre groupe a le moins de chance.* / Our group has the least luck.

Exercises

A. Adjectives – Gender

Indicate the feminine form and meaning of the following adjectives.

1. chaude

2. beau

3. pauvre

4. chanceux

5. doux

6. petit

7. favori

8. neuf

9. cher

10. bon

11. noir

12. mignon

13. facile

14. long

15. sec

16. dernier

17. faux

18. âgé

19. actif

20. paresseux

B. Adjectives – Number

Indicate the plural form and meaning of the following adjectives.

1. gentille

2. surpris

3. principal

4. heureuse

5. jaloux

6. original

7. normale

8. nouveau

9. intéressant

10. grosse

C. Adjectives – Placement

Translate the following phrases using the given nouns and adjectives.

1. a good story – bon, histoire

2. the green cars – vert, voiture

3. a pretty dress – joli, robe

4. the poor teachers – pauvre, professeur

5. a cleam bedroom – propre, chambre

6. a simple life – simple, vie

7. the expensive gifts – cher, cadeau

8. a bad decision – mauvais, décision

9. a beautiful apartment – beau, appartement

10. the large houses – grand, maison

D. Adverbs

Complete the sentence with a properly placed adverb.

1. Il joue de la guitare. / He plays the guitar very well.

2. Je ne me sens pas bien. / I don't feel well today.

3. J'ai vu ça. / I have already seen that.

4. Je leur rends souvent. / I visit them often.

5. Elle a répondu. / She answered quickly.

Answers

A.

1. chaude, hot/warm

2. belle, beautiful

3. pauvre, poor

4. chanceuse, lucky

5. douce, sweet/gentle

6. petite, small

7. favorite, favorite

8. neuve, new

9. chère, dear/expensive

10. bonne, good

11. noire, black

12. mignonne, cute

13. facile, easy

14. longue, long

15. séche, dry

16. dernière, last

17. fausse, false

18. âgée, old

19. active, active

20. paresseuse, lazy

B.

1. gentilles, nice/kind

2. surpris, surprised

3. principaux, principal

4. heureuses, happy

5. jaloux, jealous

6. originaux, original

7. normales, normal

8. nouveaux, new

9. intéressants, interesting

10. grosses, big/fat

C.

1. une bonne histoire

2. les voitures vertes

3. une jolie robe

4. les pauvres professeurs

5. une chambre propre

6. une vie simple

7. les cadeaux chers

8. une mauvaise décision

9. un bel appartement

10. les grandes maisons

D.

1. Il joue très bien de la guitare.

2. Je ne me sens pas bien aujourd'hui.

3. J'ai déjà vu ça.

4. Je leur rends assez souvent.

5. Elle a répondu rapidement.

Chapter 5: Making Sentences

A sentence is a string of words that states a complete thought. All sentences consist of a subject and a predicate. The subject is either a noun or a subject pronoun, which can be stated or in some cases, implied. The predicate tells something about the subject and is made up of a verb and an optional complement.

Subject	Verb	Complement
J' (I)	*ai pleur.* (cried.)	
Tu (You)	*seras* (will be)	*a good father.* (un bon père.)

You can see from the above examples that French and English follow the same pattern. However, when you start making more complex sentences, the word order won't always be the same.

Elements of a Sentence

In the previous chapters, you learned about the functions and how to use nouns, subject pronouns, verbs, adjectives, and adverbs. While you can compose logical sentences with only these, you need to understand the other elements to be able to effectively communicate in French.

Articles

Earlier in Chapter 2, you learned about articles. When you start making your own sentences, you'll find that you have to use these tiny words quite often. There are three types of French articles – definite, indefinite, and partitive – and their usage doesn't usually correspond to the articles in English.

Type	Masculine	Feminine	Before a Vowel	Plural
Definite	le	la	l'	les
Indefinite	un	une	un / une	des
Partitive	du (de + le)	de la	de l'	des (de + les)

The table above summarizes the different types and forms of French articles. Let's take a closer look at each type and how to properly use them.

Definite Articles

Definite articles are used to introduce a specific noun. Use this article whenever you use the in English.

- o *Nous allons à la banque.* / We're going to the bank.

- o *J'ai rendu les livres.* / I returned the book.

However, there are many instances where the is skipped but the French article should be used. Use a definite article when:

- Denoting the general sense or naming a category of a noun

  - o *L'amour est aveugle.* / Love is blind.

- Stating a preference

    o *Elle aime <u>les</u> pâtes.* / She likes pasta.

    o *Le garçon déteste <u>les</u> légumes.* / The boy hates vegetables.

- Expressing every or on + a certain day

    o *C'est fermé tous <u>les</u> mercredis.* / It's closed every Wednesday.

    o *Je ne travaille pas <u>le</u> dimanche.* / I don't work on Sundays.

- Naming a language or geographical location

    o *<u>La</u> Chine est un très grand pays.* / China is a very big country.

    o *J'étudie <u>le</u> français.* / I'm studying French.

Indefinite Articles

This type of article refers to an unspecified noun. You can use it the way you use *a, an,* and *some* in English.

    o *J'ai trouvé <u>un</u> livre.* / I found a book.

    o *Ella achètera <u>des</u> fleurs.* / She will buy some flowers.

Don't use an indefinite article when referring to someone's profession or religion, even when it's used in English.

    o *Je suis ingénieur.* / I'm an engineer.

    o *Elle veut être pilote.* / She wants to be a pilot.

Change the indefinite article to *de* when constructing a negative sentence, unless you're using the verb *être*.

- o Positive: *J'ai <u>une</u> question.* / I have a question.

- o Negative: *J'ai ne pas <u>de</u> questions.* / I don't have any questions.

Partitive Articles

This type of article corresponds to the English "some" or "any." It's used to indicate an unknown or uncountable quantity or something that's part of a whole. Partitive articles are commonly used to talk about eating or drinking something.

- o *Je veux <u>du</u> sucre dans mon café.* / I want (some) sugar in my coffee.

- o *Je vais boire <u>de l'</u>eau.* / I will drink (some) water.

Like indefinite articles, partitive articles also change to *de* when used in a negative sentence.

- o Positive: *J'ai mangé <u>de la</u> soupe.* / I ate (some) soup.

- o Negative: *Je n'ai pas mangé <u>de</u> soupe.* / I didn't eat any soup.

Pronominal Verbs

A pronominal verb is a combination of the infinitive and the reflexive pronoun *se*. To conjugate pronominal verbs, you have to make the reflexive pronoun agree with the subject and place it before the verb conjugated according to the rules described in Chapter 3.

The different forms of reflexive pronouns are as follows:

- *me (m')* – me, myself

- *te (t'), toi* – you, yourself

- *se (s')* – him, himself, her, herself, it, itself, them, themselves

- *nous* – us, ourselves

- *vous* – you, yourself, yourselves

There are three types of pronominal verbs – reflexive, reciprocal, and idiomatic.

Reflexive Verbs

These verbs indicate that the action is performed by the subject upon himself. They mostly refer to personal circumstance, part of the body, clothing, and location.

s'approcher de	to approach	s'intéresser à	to be interested in
s'asseoir	to sit down	se laver	to wash
se baigner	to bathe, swim	le lever	to get up
se brosser	to brush	se maquiller	to put on makeup
se coucher	to go to bed	se marier	to get married

se couper	to cut oneself	se moucher	to blow one's nose
se dépêcher	to hurry	se noyer	to drown
se doucher	to take a shower	se peigner	to comb one's hair
s'énerver	to get annoyed	se promener	to take a walk
s'enrhumer	to catch a cold	se raser	to shave
se fâcher	to get angry	se regarder	to look at oneself
se fatigue	to get tired	se reposer	to rest
se fier	to trust	se réveiller	to wake up
s'habiller	to get dressed	se soûler	to get drunk
s'habituer à	to get used to	se souvenir de	to remember
s'imaginer	to imagine	se taire	To be quiet

o *Nous <u>nous sommes réveillés</u> tard ce matin.* / We woke up late this worning.

o *Je <u>me lave</u> les mains.* / I'm washing my hands.

Many of the verbs listed above can also function as non-reflexive verbs when they describe the subject performing the action on someone or something else.

- *Je les <u>ai réveillés</u> tard ce matin.* / I woke them up late this morning.

- *Je <u>laverai</u> mes vêtements plus tard.* / I will wash my clothes later.

Reciprocal Verbs

Reciprocal verbs denote that two or more subjects are performing the action on one another.

s'adorer	to adore	s'embrasser	to kiss
s'aimer	to love	se parler	to talk to
s'apercevoir	to see	se promettre	to promise
se comprendre	to understand	se quitter	to leave
se connaître	to know	se regarder	to look at
se détester	to hate	se rencontrer	to meet
se dire	to tell	se sourire	to smile at
se disputer	to argue	se téléphoner	to call
s'écrire	to write to	se voir	to see

- *Nous <u>nous sommes rencontrés</u> en France.* / We met in France.

- *Ils <u>se disputent</u> toujours.* / They always argue.

As with reflexive verbs, reciprocal verbs can also be used without the pronominal pronoun and function as a non-reciprocal verb.

- o *J'ai rencontré quelqu'un d'intéressant.* / I met someone interesting.

- o *Je ne discuterai plus.* / I won't argue anymore.

Idiomatic Pronominal Verbs

These verbs have meanings that can vary depending on the presence or absence of a reflexive pronoun.

s'en aller	to go away	to go
s'amuser	to have a good time	to amuse
s'appeler	to be named	to call
s'arrêter	to stop oneself	to stop (someone or something else)
s'attendre (à)	to expect	to wait for
se demander	to wonder	to ask
se débrouiller	to manage, to get by	to disentangle
se dépêcher	to hurry	to send quickly
se diriger (vers)	to head toward	to be in charge of, to run
se douter	to suspect	to doubt

s'eclipser	to slip away	to eclipse, to overshadow
s'endormir	to fall asleep	to put to sleep
s'ennuyer	to be bored	to bother
s'entendre	to get along	to hear
se figurer	to imagine	to appear, to represent
s'inquiéter	to worry	to alarm
s'installer	to settle in	to install
se mettre à	to begin to	to place, to put
se plaindre	to complain	to pity
se rendre à	to go to	to return
se réunir	to get together	to collect, to gather
se tromper	to be mistaken	to deceive
se trouver	to be located	to find

- *Je m'appelle Alexandre.* / My name is Alexandre – *J'appelle Alexandre.* / I'm calling Alexandre.

- *Il se dirige vers le bureau.* / He's heading toward the office. – *Il dirige le bureau.* / He is running the office.

Object Complement

The object complement,or simply object, is either a noun, pronoun, or phrase, which receives the action of the verb. Within a sentence, a verb may or may not have an object. If it does have an object, the action can either be direct or indirect.

A direct objects complement answers the question "what" or "whom" the subject is acting upon. In contrast, an indirect object complement answers the question "for whom" or "to whom" the subject is doing something. While direct objects can be people, places, things, or ideas, indirect objects can only be people or other animals.

- o *J'ai donné à Ana un bouquet de roses.* / I gave Ana a bouquet of roses.

  - o Direct object: *un bouquet de roses*

  - o Indirect object: *à Ana*

- o *Je conduis une nouvelle voiture.* / I'm driving a new car.

  - o Direct object: *une nouvelle voiture*

Object Pronouns

Object pronouns replace nouns or phrases that act as nouns affected by the action of the verb. There are distinct sets of direct and indirect pronouns although only the third person singular and plural forms differ.

Direct Object Pronouns		Indirect Object Pronouns	
me	me (m')	(to) me	me (m')

you	te (t')	(to) you	te (t')
he, it	le (l')	(to) him	lui
her, it	la (l')	(to her)	lui
us	nous	(to) us	nous
you	vous	(to) you	vous
them	les	(to) them	leur

In both English and French, direct object pronouns are used when there's no need for the preposition "to" or "for" between the verb and the object. When those prepositions are used, the object is indirect.

- Direct: *Je l'ai acheté hier.* / I bought it yesterday.

- Indirect: *Il lui parle.* / He is talking to her.

Although the preposition is commonly dropped in English, it doesn't make the object direct. If you can add "to" or "for" in the sentence and the meaning is still the same, you should use an indirect pronoun.

- *Sa mère lui a acheté des chaussures.* / Her mother bought her shoes. (Her mother bought new shoes **for** her.)

Position of Object Pronouns

French object pronouns are placed before the verb they're tied to. This is straightforward when it comes to verbs in simple tense as shown in the following examples.

- *Je <u>lui montre</u> des photos.* / I'm showing him some photos.

- *Je <u>t'attendais</u>.* / I was waiting for you.

- *Il <u>le donnera</u> à Anne.* / He will give it to Anne.

In the compound past tense, the action is expressed by both the auxiliary verb and past participle so the pronoun is placed before the two.

- *Je <u>lui ai montré</u> des photos.* / I showed him some photos.

When the second verb in a compound verb is an infinitive, the object pronoun is placed before the infinitive.

- *Je vais <u>les appeler</u>.* / I'm going to call them.

- *Je voulais <u>te voir</u>.* / I wanted to see you.

Prepositions

A preposition relates two elements within a sentence. It shows a relationship of space, direction, time, or manner. The table below lists some of the most common French prepositions.

à	*ah*	to, at, in
après	*ah-preh*	after
avant	*ah-vahN*	before
avec	*ah-vehk*	with
chez	*shay*	at the house, office of

contre	*kohNtr*	against
dans	*dahN*	in
de	*duh*	from, of
depuis	*duh-pwee*	for, since
derrière	*deh-ryehr*	behind
devant	*duh-vahN*	in front of
en	*ahN*	in
entre	*ahNtr*	between, among
envers	*ahN-vehr*	toward
loin (de)	*lwaN(-duh)*	far (from)
par	*pahr*	through, by
parmi	*pahr-mee*	among
pendant	*pahN-dahN*	during
pour	*poor*	for, in order to
près (de)	*preh(-duh)*	near
sans	*sahN*	without
sauf	*sof*	except
selon	*suh-lohN*	according to
sous	*soo*	under
sur	*sewr*	on
vers	*vehr*	towards

Commonly Used Prepositions

French prepositions are quite tricky because they vary a lot from English prepositions. As you can see from the table above, some prepositions have more than one meaning and there are a few with the same English meaning. In addition, there are many instances where a preposition is required but not in English and vice versa.

Most French learners struggle with prepositions for a long time. As a beginner, it's important to focus on and understand the prepositions that you will most often use.

The preposition à

À usually means "to" but it can also mean "in" or "at." It is usually followed by a definitive article and forms the following contractions:

- à + le – au

- à + les – aux

À is used in the following:

- Going to or being in a location, a city, or a country with a masculine name

    o *Je suis <u>à la maison</u>.* / I'm (at) home.

    o *Je vais <u>au Québec</u>.* / I'm going to Quebec.

    o *Ella est <u>au Canada</u>.* / She's in Canada.

- A point in time (when at is used)

- *Nous arriverons <u>à minuit</u>.* / We'll arrive at midnight.

- *Ce garçon a commencé à marcher <u>à 10 mois</u>.* / That kid started walking at 10 months.

Note: Many common verbs must be followed by *à* (and less often *de*) before a noun or a verb in the infinitive form. There's no simple way to categorize these verbs so you'll have to familiarize yourself with these verbs that require a preposition.

- Expressing a range

  - *d'octobre à décembre* / from October to November

- Distance in space or time

  - *Vous êtes <u>à deux kilomètres</u>.* / You're two kilometers away.

  - *Nous vivons <u>à une heure de la plage</u>.* / We live an hour from the beach.

The preposition de

De usually means "from" or "of." When following by a definite article, it forms the following contractions:

- de + le – du

- de + lex – des

Usage of *de* is the same as how "from" and "of" are used in English. However, *de* is also commonly used to show possession.

> o *C'est la maison de Jean.* / That is Jean's house.

Many verbs also require *de* in front of a noun or an infinitive.

> o *Tu as oublié de fermer la porte.* / You forgot to close the door.

> o *Nous vous remercions d'être venus.* / We thank you for coming.

The preposition en

En usually means "in" but it can mean many things in French. It is used in the following:

- Means of motorized transport

> o *Nous avons voyagé en bus.* / We travelled by bus.

- Saying like or as when doing something

> o *Cet homme agit en enfant.* / That man acts like a child.

> o *Je suis venu ici en ami.* / I came here as a friend.

- Going to or in a country whose name is feminine or begins with a vowel

> o *Ils sont en Pologne.*

> o *Nous allons en Israël.* / We're going to Israel.

Stressed Pronouns

Prepositions can be followed by pronouns and when they do, stressed pronouns are used. There are nine forms of French stressed pronouns.

me	moi	us	nous
you	toi	you	vous
him	lui	them (m.)	eux
her	elle	them (f.)	elles

- ○ *Je partirai <u>sans eux</u>.* / I will leave without them.

- ○ *Il se tient <u>devant moi</u>.* / He's standing in front of me.

- ○ *Ils courent <u>vers toi</u>.* / They're running toward you.

Stressed pronouns also replace indirect object pronouns referring to persons when certain French verbs and expressions are used. These verbs do not allow indirect object pronouns to precede them.

en appeler à	to appeal to, address
avoir affaire à	to have to deal with
croire à	to believe in
être à	to belong to
faire attention à	to pay attention to

s'habituer à	to get used to
penser à	to think of/about
renoncer à	to give up/renounce
revenir à	to come back to
rêver à	to dream of
songer à	to think/dream of
tenir à	to be fond of, care about
venir à	to come to

- ○ *Je pense à toi tous les jours.* / I think of you everyday.

- ○ *Vous pouvez venir à moi n'importe quand.* / You can come to me anytime.

The Pronouns *y* and *en*

Sometimes, you need to replace a prepositional phrase in a sentence especially if you're giving an answer to a question. When you have to do that, you need to use the adverbial pronouns *y* and *en*. These tiny words allow you to avoid repeating words and have a conversation that sounds normal.

- • Use *y* to replace prepositional phrases indicating location except when the preposition is *de*.

- ○ *Je vais à la plage.* / I'm going to the beach. – *J'y vais.*

- *Nous sommes dans le bâtiment.* / We're in the building. – *Nous y sommes.*

- You can also use *y* to replace à + any non-person noun.

  - *Je pense à mon avenir.* / I'm thinking about my future. – *J'y pense.*

- Use en to replace a prepositional phrase that indicates a location and starts with the preposition *de.*

  - *Nous revenons de la bibliothèque.* / We're coming back from the library. – *Nous en revenons.*

- *En* can also be used to replace *de* + indefinite article + noun.

  - *Nous buvons du thé.* / We're drinking some tea. – *Nous en buvons.*

Note: You can find *y* in various expressions such as *il y a* (there is) and *allons-y* (let's go). It doesn't mean that it's replacing something since these are fixed expressions.

Adjectives

Adjectives not only describe characteristics; they also have a few other grammatical functions.

Demonstrative Adjectives

Demonstrative adjectives indicate which noun or pronoun is being referred to in a sentence. In English, demonstratives are "this," "that," "these," and "those." The French language also has four demonstratives but their meanings and functions aren't exactly the same.

- ***cet*** – for masculine singular nouns beginning with a vowel or vowel sound

- ***ce*** – for masculine singular nouns beginning with a consonant

- ***cette*** – for all feminine nouns

- ***ces*** – for all plural nouns

The demonstratives agree in gender and number with the noun they modify. However, they can't differentiate between "this/that" and "these/those" on their own. To make a distinction, hyphenate *-ci* to the noun if you mean this or these and *-la* if you want to say that or those.

- *Je veux lire ce livre-ci.* / I want to read this book.

- *Cette maison-la est énorme.* / That house is huge.

- *Ces fleurs-ci sont belles.* / These flowers are beautiful.

- *Je vais acheter ces chaussures-la.* / I will buy those shoes.

Possesive Adjectives

Possesive adjectives replace the article to indicate ownership. It is placed before the noun or the adjective if there's one that precedes the noun. French possesive adjectives have several forms since it has to agree with the number and gender of the possessed noun.

	Masculine	Feminine	Plural
my	mon	ma	mes
your	ton	ta	tes
his, her	son	sa	ses
our	notre		nos
vous	votre		vos
their	leur		leurs

- *Mes chiens sont très mignons.* / My dogs are very cute.

- *Il veut voir notre nouvelle maison.* / He wants to see our new house.

Remember that possesive adjectives agree with the modified or possessed noun. The gender and number of the owner does not affect the form of the adjective to be used

- *sa mere* / his mother

- *tes enfants* / your children

- *son frère* / her brother

A possessive adjective and the noun (and adjective) it modifies can be replaced by an article + possesive pronoun. The table that follows shows the different forms of this combination.

English	Masc. Singular	Fem. Singular	Masc. Plural	Fem. Plural
mine	le mien	la mienne	les miens	les miennes
yours (*tu*)	le tien	la tienne	les tiens	les tiennes
his, hers, its	le sien	la sienne	les siens	les siennes
ours	le nôtre	la nôtre	les nôtres	
yours (*vous*)	le vôtre	la vôtre	les vôtres	
theirs	le leur	la leur	les leurs	

As with possessive adjectives, possessive pronouns must agree in gender and number of the possessed and not the owner.

- o *Cette maison est la nôtre.* / This house is ours.

- o *Ces sont les miens.* / These (clothes) are mine.

Note: When an action refers to one's own body parts, a definitive article (paired with a pronominal verb) is usually used instead of possesive adjective.

- o *Le garçon se brosse les dents.* / The boy is brushing his teeth.

- o *Elle se brosse les cheveux.* / She's brushing her hair.

Types of Sentences

There are four types of sentences: *phrase declarative* (statement), *phrase interrogative* (question), *phrase exclamative* (exclamation), and *phrase imperative* (command).

Declarative Sentence

The declarative is the most commonly used type of sentence. It can be expressed in an affirmative or negative manner. Almost all of the examples you have previously encountered in this book are affirmative declarative sentences so by now, you should be familiar with its construction.

Expressing a Negative Statement

You can easily transform an affirmative to a negative sentence by sandwiching the verb between negative French words – *ne* and *pas*.

- *Je ne sais pas.* / I don't know.

- *Je n'aime pas les pâtes.* / I don't like pasta.

In the compound past and near-future tenses, *ne* and *pas* surrounds only the first verb.

- *Je n'ai pas encore vu ce film.* / I haven't seen that movie yet.

- *Je ne vais pas voyager bientôt.* / I'm not going to travel soon.

If there's an object pronoun, the pronoun is also sandwiched between the negative words.

o *Nous ne le faisons pas aujourd'hui.* / We're not doing it today.

o *Je ne t'ai pas donné ça.* / I didn't give you that.

Ne doesn't translate to anything in English but *pas* means "not." You can use the following negative words to replace *pas* in a sentence.

aucun/aucune + noun	no, none, not any
jamais	never
même pas	not even
ni … ni	neither … nor
nulle part	nowhere
pas encore	not yet
pas grand-chose	not much
pas non plus	either, neither
personne	nobody, no one
plus	no longer, not any more
rien	nothing

o *Elle ne dirait jamais ça.* / She would never say that.

o *Je ne peux plus attendre.* / I can't wait any more.

o *Nous n'allons nulle part.* / We're not going anywhere.

166

When the subject of a sentence is a negative word, add *ne* before the verb.

- o *Aucun de nous ne voulait ça.* / None of us wanted that.

- o *Rien ne peut être fait.* / Nothing can be done.

Finally, here are some negative expressions that you can use during conversations.

- o *Jamais plus.* / Never again.

- o *Moi non plus.* / Me neither.

- o *Pas du tout.* / Not at all.

- o *Pas grand*-chose. / Not much.

- o *Pas maintenant.* / Not now.

- o *Pas question.* / No way.

The Passive Voice

Normally, the subject of a sentence is the performer of the action described by the verb. This is known as the active voice. It's also possible for the receiver of the action to become the subject. This sentence construction is called the passive voice.

The tone of the French passive voice is a bit formal and literary so it's commonly used in conversations. However, there are instances when you may need to use the passive voice:

- • You want to put the emphasis on the receiver of the action

- *Vous avez encore été trompé par eux.* / You were fooled by them again.

- You don't know the performer of the action or the performer is insignificant

  - *Mon téléphone a été volé.* / My phone was stolen.

  - *J'ai été vire.* / I have been fired.

The passive voice is expressed using the conjugated form of *être* and past participle of the verb describing the action. As in the compound past tense, the past participle must agree with the subject in gender and number.

- Present: *Le mur est peint.* / The wall is painted.

- Compound past: *Les murs ont été peints hier.* / The walls were painted yesterday.

- Imperfect: *La fille était surveillée par sa sœur aînée.* / The girl is being watched by her older sister.

- Simple future: *Les filles seront surveillées par leur sœur aînée.* / The girls will be watched by their older sister.

- Near-future: *Le mur va bientôt être peint.* / The wall is going to be painted soon.

You can see from the examples above that when the active voice uses compound verbs, there are three verbs in the passive voice and *être* is placed between the two verbs. Also note that the performer of the action is introduced by *par*. When the verb expresses a state of being instead of action, the performer, if present, is introduced by *de*.

- o *Elle est aimée de tout le monde.* / She is loved by everyone.

- o *Il est détesté de mis amis.* / He is hated by my friends.

Interrogative Sentence

When you ask questions, you use interrogative sentences. They're either yes/no or information questions.

Yes/No Questions

The easiest way to ask a question when the answer you're looking for is simply yes or no is raising the pitch of your voice at the end of a declarative sentence. In written form, the structure of the sentence doesn't change except for the punctuation mark.

- o *C'est correct.* / It's correct. – *C'est correct?* / Is it correct?

Other ways of asking yes/no questions are using the question tags *n'est-ce pas* and *est-ce que* or through inversion.

N'est-ce pas?

N'est-ce pas (*nehs pas*) literally translates to isn't that so. This question tag is added at the end of a declarative sentence to make it a question.

- o *Ils travaillent aujourd'hui, n'est-ce pas?* / They're working today, aren't they?

- o *Vous n'êtes pas en colère, n'est-ce pas?* / You're not angry, are you?

Est-ce que

Placing *est-ce que* (*esh-kuh*) at the start of a declarative sentence turns it into a question. While it literally means "is it that," it's not translated or it's interpreted in a different way in English. This method is commonly used in everyday spoken French.

- o *Est-ce que tu fâché contre moi?* / Are you mad at me?

- o *Est-ce que tu nes comprends pas ça?* / Don't you understand that?

Inversion

By reversing the order of the subject pronoun and the conjugated verb and joining the two words with a hyphen, a statement becomes a question.

- o *Voulez-vous des pommes?* / Do you want some apples?

- o *Ne savent-ils pas?* / Don't they know?

- When the subject pronoun is *il* or *elle* and the verb ends in a vowel, a *t* is added in between to avoid having two vowels next to each other.

  - o *Aimé-t-il son nouvel appartement?* / Does he love his new apartment?

Note that inversion with *je* is rarely used and should be avoided. Inversion also applies only to pronouns and never to nouns.

Inversion isn't merely switching the pronoun and verb. There are a lot more rules involved especially when the subject is a noun or the verb is a compound type. However, since inversion is commonly used in written French and formal conversations, you can stick with the other much simple ways of asking yes/no qustions.

Giving an Answer

If your answer to a question is "no," use *non*. If your answer is "yes," choose between *oui* and *si*.

- Use *oui* when answering yes to an affirmative question.

    o *Tu parles français?* / Do you speak French? - *Oui, je parle français.* / Yes, I speak French.

- Use *si* when answering yes to a negative question.

    o *Tu ne me connais pas?* / Don't you know me? – *Si, je te connais.* / Yes, I know you.

Information Questions

When the answer you're looking for is more than just a "yes" or "no," you need to use question words so the listener will know that you're asking for certain information. Question words are either pronouns, adjectives, or adverbs and are usually placed at the beginning of a sentence.

French	Pronunciation	English
qui	*kee*	who, whom
que, qu'est-ce que	*kuh, kehs-kuh*	what

quand	*kahN*	when
où	*oo*	where
comment	*kohN-mahN*	how
pourquoi	*poor-kwah*	why
à quelle heure	*ah-kehl-uhr*	at what time
à qui	*ah-kee*	to whom
à quoi	*ah-kwah*	to what
avec qui	*ah-vehk-kee*	with whom
avec quoi	*ah-vehk-kwah*	with what
de qui	*duh-kee*	of, about, from whom
combien (de + noun)	*kohN-byaN (duh)*	how much, how many
d' où	*doo*	from where
quel + noun	*kehl*	what, which

Note: Avoid confusing *où* with *ou*. The latter means *or* in English.

There are several ways of asking a question using question words. In both formal and informal spoken French, the question word is often combined with *est-ce que* to indicate that a question is being asked and avoid being misheard by the listener. It's also simpler because it doesn't involve inversion.

- *Qu'est-ce que tu fais?* / What are you doing?

- *Où est-ce que tu as mis le chocolat?* / Where did you put the chocolate?

- *Quand est-ce que ils vont arriver?* / When will they arrive?

- *Qui est-ce que a pris mon chocolat?* / Who took my chocolate?

- *Comment est-ce que le chat est rentré là-dedans?* / How did the cat get in there?

- *Pourquoi est-ce que tu as mangé mon chocolat?* / Why did you eat my chocolate?

- If the verb used in the question is only *être*, you need to add *il est* after *est-ce-que*.

  - *Où est-ce qu'il est mon chocolat?* / Where's my chocolate?

- Use *est-ce qui* instead of *est-ce que* when the answer to your question is the subject of the verb. This only applies to question words *qui* and *que*.

  - *Qu'est-ce qui vous fait le plue peur?* / What scares you the most?

  - *Qui est-ce qui t'inspire?* / Who inspires you?

- *Quel* is an interrogative adjective so it needs to agree with the gender and number of what it refers to.

- *Quelle est ta couleur préféré?* /What's your favorite color?

- *Quelles chaussures te plaisent le plus?* / Which shoes do you like best?

Imperative Sentence

The imperative usually expresses a command or order. It's also used to make a request, express a desire, recommend something, or give advice. This type of sentence uses the imperative form of the verb and the subject is often implied.

The Imperative

The imperative has three forms which correspond to the first person plural (*nous*), second person singular (*tu*), and second person plural (*vous*). The imperative of regular verbs is usually the same as the present tense form corresponding to the subject.

- For -*er* verbs, the final *s* of the *tu* form is dropped unless its followed by *en* or *y*.

    - *Donnons-leur quelque chose.* / Let's give them something.

    - *Donne-moi ton numéro.* / Give me your number.

    - *Donnez moi ce que je veux.* / (You both) Give me what I want.

- For regular -*ir* and -*re* verbs, the present tense is used.

- There are three often-used verbs with irregular imperative forms.

	Avoir	Être	Savoir
tu	aie	sois	sache
nous	ayons	soyons	sachons
vous	ayez	soyez	sachez

- o *S'il vous plaît, sache où se trouve la sortie.* / Please know where the exit is.

- o *Soyons amis.* / Let's be friends.

- o *Ayez pitié de nous.* / (You all) Have mercy on us.

- The negative command is formed by wrapping the imperative with *ne* and *pas*.

  - o *Ne viens pas ici.* / Don't come here.

Placement of Pronouns

In many instances, the imperative has an object pronoun. The position of pronoun in a command depends on whether it is affirmative or negative.

- The object pronoun is placed after the verb in an affirmative command. They are joined together with a hyphen.

  - o *Aide-nous.* / Help us.

- The object pronoun is placed after *ne* and before the verb in a negative command.

  - o *Ne lui dis pas.* / Don't tell her.

- If the imperative has both direct and indirect objects, the direct object pronounss always precede the indirect object pronouns.

    o *Montrons-<u>le-leur</u>.* / Let's show it to them.

    o *S'il vous plaît <u>ne le lui donne pas</u>.* / Please don't give it to him.

Exclamatory Sentence

To express enthusiasm, surprise, or any intense emotion, you use an exclamatory sentence. In most cases, it doesn't differ from a declarative or imperative sentence except for the punctuation mark used or in conversations, how the speaker expresses it.

    o *Je ne t'aime plus!* / I don't love you anymore!

    o *Fais-moi sortir d'ici!* / Get me out of here.

There are also exclamative words that you can use to when expressing strong emotions.

- To emphasize nouns, use the exclamative adjective *quel.*

    o *Quelle belle journée!* / What a beautiful day!

    o *Quels imbéciles!* / What fools!

- To emphasize an adjective, use the exclamative adverbs *que* or *comme.* These two are interchangeable and both can mean what or how. However, you can't skip *c'est* (it is) even though it doesn't get translated in English.

    o *Que c'est fou!* / How crazy!

o *Comme c'est beau!* / How beautiful!

The table below lists some of the most commonly used exclamations. Most of these are considered mild slang and don't translate literally in English.

French	Meaning
Allez!	Oh, c'mon!
Assez de bêtises!	Knock it off!
Bien sur!	Of course!
Bon débarras!	Good riddance!
C'est beaucoup!	That's a lot!
Cela dépasse le bornes!	That's going too far!
C'est le cas de le dire!	You can say that again!
C'est nul!	That sucks!
C'est trop fort!	You're too much!
Ça, c'est le comble!	That's the last straw!
Ça me fait rager!	That infuriates me!
Ça m'inquiète!	That bugs me!
Ça suffit!	Cut it out!
Comme c'est triste!	How sad!
Décide-toi!	Make up your mind!

(Ferme) ta gueule!	Shut up!
Grâce au ciel!	Thank heavens!
Honte à toi!	Shame on you!
J'en ai marre!	I've had it up to here!
Je n'en reviens pas!	I can't get over it!
Laisse-moi tranquille!	Leave me alone!
Mêle-toi de tes affaires!	Mind your own business!
N'importe!	Never mind!
Pas question!	No way!
Quelle chance/malchance!	How lucky/unlucky!
Quelle horreur!	How horrible!
Quel travail!	That's a lot of work!
Quel soulagement!	How sad!
Ras le bol!	I'm really fed up!
Reste couvert!	Keep your shirt on!
Tu me rends fou (folle)!	You're driving me nuts!
Tu parles!	Big deal! / You must be kidding!
Un peu!	You bet!
Va-t'en!	Go away!

Propositions and Complex Sentences

At the beginning of this chapter, you learned that a sentence consists of an expressed or implied subject, a verb, and an optional complement. In French grammar, this group of words is considered a proposition.

A *proposition* or clause can be a whole or a part of a sentence containing a verb. The conjugated verb is the core of the proposition and all the other words are grammatically related to that verb. A sentence can have one or more propositions.

There are three types of French proposition: independent, main, and subordinate.

Independent Proposition

As the name suggests, this type of proposition doesn't depend on another proposition and no other proposition depends on it. All the sample sentences that have been presented in this chapter are independent propositions.

An independent proposition can be attached to another using coordinating conjunctions. Below is a list of these conjunctions.

car	because, for	*et*	and	*ou*	or
donc	so	*mais*	but	*ou bien*	or else
ensuite	next	*or*	now, yet	*puis*	then `

A sentence can have as many independent propositions joined by a conjunction.

- *Je suis médecin et il est ingénieur.* / I'm a doctor and he's and engineer.

- *Ce n'est pas mon travail mais je le ferai quand même.* / It's not my job but I'll still do it.

Main Proposition

This type is just like an independent proposition because it also doesn't depend on other propositions. However, it has at least one subordinate proposition depending on it.

- *Son chien dormait quand il est arrivé.* / His dog was sleeping when he arrived.

  - main proposition: *Son chien dormait*

  - subordinate clause: *quand il est arrivé.*

Subordinate Proposition

Also called a dependent clause, the subordinate proposition can't stand on its own because it starts with a subordinating conjunction. In the example above, the subordinate clause is missing some information (which is found in the main clause) so its meaning is incomplete.

Subordinating Conjunctions

The table below lists some of the most commonly used subordinating conjuctions and example sentences.

- *puisque, comme* (as, since) - *Je vais le fair puisque vous ne pouvez pas.* / I'll do it since you can't.

- *lorsque, quand* (when) – *Nous allons commencer <u>quand il arrive</u>.* / We will start when he arrives.

- *que* (that) – *J'ai perdu la robe <u>que nous avons achetée hier</u>.* / I lost the dress that I bought yesterday.

- *si* (if) – *<u>Si vous voulez nous rejoindr</u>, vous devez signer ce document.* / If you want to join us, you have to sign this paper.

There are a number of phrases that function as subordinating conjuctions. The phrases listed below require a subjunctive verb when used in a subordinate proposition. Expressions marked with an asterisk also require the non-negative *ne*.

à condition que	provided that
afin que	so that
à moins que *	unless
à supposer que	assuming that
avant que *	before
bien que	although
de façon que	in such a way that
en attendant que	while, until
encore que	even though
pour que	so that
quoi que	no matter what,

	whatever
sans que *	without
supposé que	supposing

o *Je suis parti tôt <u>pour qu</u>'il ne me <u>voie</u> pas.* / I left early so that he won't see me.

o *Elle est arrivée <u>avant qu</u>'il <u>ne ferme</u> la porte à clé.* / She arrived before he locked the door.

Exercises

A. Pronominal Verbs

Complete the following sentences using the correct conjugated pronominal verb.

1. Il (s'asseoir) à côté de moi. / He sat beside me.

2. Je (se soûler) la nuit dernière. / I got drunk last night.

3. Ils (se rencontrer) l'année dernière. / They met last year

4. Tu (se plaindre) beaucoup. / You complain a lot.

5. Vous (se tromper) tous les deux. / You're both mistaken.

B. Object Pronouns

Complete the following sentences with the correct word and placement of object pronouns.

1. Je vais donner à mon voisin. / I will give them to my neighbor.

2. Il veut voir. / He wants to see us.

3. Mon chien a mangé. / My dog ate it.

4. Tu vas aimer. / You're going to love me.

5. Il déteste. / He hates you.

C. Prepositions

Translate the following phrases.

1. according to him

2. at noon

3. five kilometers away

4. behind you

5. by plane

6. in India

7. with us

8. without me

9. to Canada

10. Anne's car

D. Negative Sentence

Convert the following sentences from affirmative to negative.

1. Je vais acheter de la nourriture.

2. J'ai acheté des pommes.

3. Nous les aimons.

4. Il va le manger.

5. Elle l'a appelé.

E. Interrogative Sentences

Complete the following sentences with the correct question word and *est-ce que*/est-ce qui.

1. _____ tu cuisines? / What are you cooking?

2. _____ vous avez appelé? / When did you call?

3. _____ l'a volé? / Who stole it?

4. _____ tu es? / Where are you?

5. _____ tu fais ça? / How do you do that?

Answers

A.

1. s'est assis
2. me suis saoulé
3. se sont rencontrés
4. te plains
5. vous trompez

B.

1. vais les donner
2. veut nous voir
3. l'a mangé
4. vas m'aimer
5. te déteste

C.

1. selon lui
2. à midi
3. à cinq kilomètres
4. derrière toi
5. en avion
6. en Inde

7. avec nous

8. sans moi

9. au Canada

10. la voiture d'Anne

D.

1. Je ne vais pas acheter de la nourriture.

2. Je n'ai pas acheté de pommes.

3. Nous ne les aimons pas.

4. Il ne va pas le manger.

5. Elle ne l'a pas appelé.

E.

1. Qu'est-ce que

2. Quand est-ce que

3. Qui est-ce qui

4. Où est-ce qu'il

5. Comment est-ce que

Chapter 6: Everyday Words and Expressions

Greetings, Meeting People and General Conversations

- *Bonjour!* - Hello! / Good morning!

- *Bonsoir!* – Hello! / Good evening!

- *Salut!* – Bye! / Hi! (when seeing someone again later in the day)

- *Âllo!* – Hello! (when answering the phone)

- *Merci.* – Thank you.

- *Je vous en prie. / De rien.* – You're welcome.

- *Ça fait longtemps, dis donc.* – It's been a while. / Long time no see.

- *(Comment) ça va?* – How are you?

- *Comment allez-vous?* – How are you?

- *Quoi de neuf?* – What's up?

- *Je vais bien, merci.* – I'm fine, thank you.

- *Tres bien.* – Very well.

- *Comme ci, comme ça.* – So-so.

- *Pas mal.* – Not bad.

- *Et vous?* – What about you?

- *À bientôt. / À plus.* – See you later.

- *À demain.* – See you tomorrow.

- *Au revoir.* – Goodbye.

- *Ciao!* – See you!

- *Prenez soins de vous. / Prends soins de toi. (informal)* – Take care.

- *Enchanté(e).* – Nice meeting you.

- *Au plaisir de vous revoir.* – Hope to see you again.

- *Je suis désolé.* – I'm sorry.

- *S'il vous plaît.* – Please.

- *Bonne chance.* – Good luck.

- *Bon anniversaire!* – Happy birthday!

- *Félicitations!* – Congratulations!

- *Madame / Mme* – Madam / Mrs.

- *Mademoiselle / Mlle* – Miss

- *Monsieur / M.* - Mister / Mr. / Sir

Everyday Idiomatic Expressions

These expressions have meanings which are not the literal translation of the words. They will allow you to speak French like a native speaker. To use these expressions, simply conjugate the verb so that it agrees with the subject.

- o apprendre par cœer – to memorize
- o avoir … ans – to be … years old
- o avoir besoin de – to need
- o avoir chaud – to be warm
- o avoir envie de – to feel like
- o avoir faim – to be hungry
- o avoir froid – to be cold
- o avoir peur (de) – to be afraid of
- o avoir raison – to be right
- o avoir soif – to be thirsty
- o avoir tort – to be wrong
- o avoir de la chance – to be lucky
- o être à – to belong to
- o être d'accord (avec) – to agree (with)
- o être sur le point de – to be about to
- o y être – to understand
- o faire attention (à) – to pay attention (to)
- o faire une promenade – to take a walk

- o   faire une voyage – to take a trip

- o   n'en pouvoir plus – to be exhausted

- o   valoir mieux – to be better

- o   venir de – to have just

- o   vouloir dire – to mean

Talking About the Weather

- o   *Quel temps fait-il?* / What's the weather.

- o   *Il fait ...* / It's (The weather is) ...

  - o   *beau* / beautiful

  - o   *chaud* / hot

  - o   *du soleil* / sunny

  - o   *frais* / cool

  - o   *froid* / cold

  - o   *mauvais* / bad (nasty)

  - o   *des éclairs* / lightning

  - o   *du tonnerre* / thundering

  - o   *humide* / humid

- o   *Il y a du brouillard.* / It's foggy.

- o   *Il y a des nuages.* / It's cloudy.

- o   *Le ciel est couvert.* / It's overcast.

- *Il y a de la grêle.* / There's hail.

- *Il y a des giboulées.* / There are sudden showers.

- *Il y a des rafales.* / There are gusts of wind.

- *Il y a du vent.* / It's windy.

- *Il pleut.* / It's raining.

- *Il neige.* / It's snowing.

Family Members

aunt	la tante	*lah-tahNt*
brother	le frère	*luh-frehr*
cousin (female)	la cousine	*lah-koo-zeen*
cousin (male)	le cousin	*luh-koo-zaN*
daughter	la fille	*lah-fee-y*
daughter-in-law	la belle-fille	*lah-bell-fee-y*
father	le père	*luh-pehr*
father-in-law	le beau- père	*luh-bo-pehr*
grandchild	le petit-enfant	*luh-puh-tee-tahN-fahN*
granddaughter	la petite-fille	*la-puh-tee-fee-y*
grandfather	le grand-père	*luh-grahN-pehr*
grandmother	la grand-mère	*lah-grahN-mehr*

grandson	le petit-fils	*luh-puh-tee-fees*
husband	le mari	*luh-mah-ree*
mother	la mère	*lah-mehr*
mother-in-law	la belle-mère	*lah-behl-mehr*
nephew	le neveu	*luh-nuh-vuh*
niece	la nièce	*lah-nyehs*
sister	la sœur	*lah-suhr*
son	le fils	*luh-fees*
son-in-law	le gendre	*luh-zhahNdr*
stepbrother	le demi-frère	*luh-duh-mee-frehr*
stepdaughter	la belle-fille	*lah-behl-fee-y*
stepsister	la demi-sœur	*lah-duh-mee-suhr*
stepson	le beau-fils	*luh-bo-fees*
uncle	l'oncle	*lohNkl*
wife	la femme	*lah-fehm*

Pets and Animals

domestic animals	les animaux domestiques	*lay-zah-nee-mo-doh-meh-steek*
dog	le chien	*luh-shyaN*
cat	le chat	*luh-shah*
rabbit	le lapin	*luh-lah-paN*
goldfish	le poisson rouge	*luh-pwah-sohN-roozh*
fish	les poissons	*lay-pwah-sohN*
hamster	le hamster	*luh-ahN-stehr*
snake	le serpent	*luh-sehr-pahN*
mouse	la souris	*lah-soo-ree*
bird	l'oiseau	*lwah-so*
farm animals	les animaux de la ferme	*lay-zah-nee-mo-duh-lah-fehr*
pig	le cochon	*luh-koh-shohN*
cow	la vache	*lah-vahsh*
chicken	la poule	*lah-pool-uh*
goat	la chèvre	*lah-shehvr*
horse	le cheval	*luh-shuh-vahl*

donkey	l'âne *m.*	*lahn*
duck	le canard	*luh-kah-nahr*
wild animals	les animaux sauvages	*lay-zah-nee-mo-so-vahzh*
deer	le cerf	*luh-sehrf*
hawk	le faucon	*luh-fo-kohN*
eagle	l'aigle *m.*	*lehgl*
tiger	le tigre	*luh-teegr*
lion	le lion	*luh-lyohN*
elephant	l'éléphant *m.*	*lay-lay-phahN*
giraffe	la girafe	*lah-zhee-rahf*
monkey	le singe	*luh-saNzh*
gorilla	le gorille	*luh-goh-ree-yuh*
zebra	le zèbre	*luh-zehbr*
antelope	l'antilope *f.*	*l'ahN-tee-lohp*
kangaroo	le kangourou	*luh-kahN-goo-roo*
insects	les insectes	*lay-zaN-sehkt*
ant	la fourmi	*lah-foor-mee*
spider	l'araignée *f.*	*lah-reh-nyay*
butterfly	le papillon	*luh-pah-pyohN*

housefly	la mouche	*lah-moosh*
mosquito	le moustique	*luh-moo-steek*
bee	l'abeille *f.*	*lah-beh-y*
wasp	la guêpe	*lah-gehp*
ladybug	la coccinelle	*lah-kohk-see-nehl*

At Home

attic	le grenier	*luh-gruh-nyay*
balcony	le balcon	*luh-bahl-kohN*
bathroom	la salle de bains	*lah-sahl-duh-baN*
bedroom	la chambre	*lah-shahNbr*
cellar	la cave	*lah-kahv*
dining room	la salle à manger	*lah-sahl-ah-mahN-zhay*
door	la porte	*lah-pohrt*
entrance	l'entrée *f.*	*lahN-tray*
garage	le garage	*luh-gah-razh*
garden	le jardin	*luh-zhahr-daN*
guest room	la chambre d'amis	*lah-shahNbr-dah-mee*
kitchen	la cuisine	*lah-kwee-zeen*

living room	le salon	*luh-sah-lohN*
restroom	les toilettes	*lay-twah-leht*
roof	le toit	*luh-twah*
stairs	l'escalier *m.*	*leh-skah-lyay*
terrace	la terrasse	*lah-teh-rahs*
window	la fenêtre	*lah-feh-nehtr*
yard	la cour	*lah-koor*

Furniture and Accessories

armchair	le fauteuil	*luh-fo-tuh-y*
bathroom sink	le lavabo	*luh-lah-vah-bo*
bathtub	la baignoire	*lah-beh-nywahr*
bed	le lit	*luh-lee*
bedspread	le couvre-lit	*luh-koo-vruh-lee*
chair	la chaise	*lah-shehs*
chandelier	le lustre	*luh-lewstr*
closet	le placard	*luh-plah-kahr*
comforter	l'édredon *m.*	*leh-druh-dohN*
couch	le divan	*luh-dee-vahN*
curtain	le rideau	*luh-ree-do*

desk	le bureau	*luh-bew-ro*
double bed	le grand lit	*luh-grahN-lee*
dresser	la commode	*lah-koh-mohd*
kitchen sink	l'évier *m.*	*lay-vyay*
lamp	la lampe	*lah-lahNp*
mirror	le miroir	*luh-mee-rwahr*
nigthstand	la table de chevet	*lah-tahbl-duh-shuh-veh*
piece of furniture	le meuble	*luh-muhbl*
pillow	l'oreiller	*loh-reh-yay*
rug	le tapis	*luh-tah-pee*
shade	le store	*luh-stohr*
shelves	l'étagère	*lay-tah-zhehr*
shutter	le volet	*luh-voh-leh*
sofa	le sofa	*luh-soh-fah*
throw pillow	le coussin	*luh-koo-saN*
wallpaper	le papier peint	*luh-pah-pyay-pehn*

Household Appliances

blender	le mixeur	*luh-meeks-uhr*
burner	la plaque de cuisson	*lah-plahk-duh-kwee-sohN*
dishwasher	le lave-vaisselle	*luh-lahv-veh-sehl*
dryer	le sèche-linge	*luh-sehsh-laNzh*
fan	le ventilateur	*luh-vahN-tee-lah-tuhr*
food processor	le robot cuisine	*luh-roh-bo-kwee-zeen*
freezer	le congélateur	*luh-kohN-zhay-lah-tuhr*
garbage disposal	le vide-ordures	*luh-veed-ohr-dewr*
hair dryer	le sèche-cheveux	*luh-sehsh-shuh-vuh*
microwave oven	le micro-ondes	*luh-mee-kro-ohNd*
fridge	le frigo	*luh-free-go*
stove	la cuisinière	*lah-kwee-zee-nyehr*
toaster	le grille-pain	*luh-greel-pehn*
washing machine	la machine à laver	*lah-mah-sheen-ah-lah-vay*
water heater	le chauffe-eau	*luh-shof-o*

Daily Routines

brush the teeth	se brosser les dents	*suh-brossay-lay-dahN*
clean the house	faire le ménage	*fehr-luh-may-nahzh*
cook	faire la cuisine	*fehr-lah-kwee-zeen*
eat breakfast	prendre le petit déjeuner	*prahNdr-luh-puh-tee-day-zhuh-nay*
eat dinner	dîner	*dee-nay*
eat lunch	déjeuner	*day-zhuh-nay*
empty the garbage can	vider la poubelle	*vee-day-lah-poo-behl*
feed the cat	donner à manger au chat	*doh-nay-ah-mahn-zhay-o-shah*
get up	se lever	*suh-leh-vay*
go home	rentrer à la maison	*rahN-tray-ah-lah-meh-sohN*
go to bed	se coucher	*suh-koo-shay*
go to the gym	aller au gymnase	*ah-lay-o-zheem-nahs*
go to work	aller au travail	*ah-lay-o-trah-vahy*
groom oneself	faire sa toilette	*fehr-sah-twah-leht*
have a coffee	boire un café	*bwahr-uhN-kah-fay*

have a snack	prendre un goûter	*prahNdr-uhN-goo-tay*
hurry	se dépêcher	*suh-day-peh-shay*
listen to music	écouter de la musique	*ay-koo-tay-duh-lah-mew-zeek*
make phone calls	téléphoner	*tay-lay-foh-nay*
make the bed	faire le lit	*fehr-luh-lee*
meet friends	retrouver des amis	*reh-troo-vay-deh-zah-mee*
prepare dinner	préparer le dîner	*pray-pah-ray-luh-dee-nay*
rest	se reposer	*suh-reh-poh-say*
take a shower	prendre une douche	*prahNdr-ewn-doosh*
wake up	se réveiller	*suh-ray-veh-yay*
walk the dog	promener le chien	*proh-meh-nay-luh-shyaN*
wash the dishes	laver la vaisselle	*lah-vay-lah-vah-sehl*
wash the laundry	faire la lessive	*fehr-lah-leh-seev*
water the plants	arroser les plantes	*ah-roh-zay-lay-plahNt*

At Work

assistant	le assistant	*luh-ah-see-stahN*
boss	le patron	*luh-pah-trohN*
coworker	le collègue	*luh-koh-lehg*
company	la entreprise	*lah-ahN-treh-preez*
computer	le ordinateur	*luh-ohr-dee-nah-tuhr*
email	le courriel	*luh-koo-ryehl*
employee	le employe	*luh-ahN-plwah-yay*
garbage can	la poubelle	*lah-poo-behl*
job	le emploi	*luh-ahN-plwah*
laptop	le portable	*luh-pohr-tahbl*
manager	le responsable	*luh-rehs-pohN-sahbl*
office, desk*	le bureau	*luh-bew-ro*
office supplies	les fournitures de bureau	*lay-foor-nee-tewr-duh-bew-ro*
pen	le stylo	*luh-stee-lo*
pencil	le crayon	*luh-krah-yohN*
printer	la imprimante	*lah-aN-pree-maNt*
salary	le salaire	*luh-sah-lehr*

secretary	le secrétaire	*luh-seh-kray-tehr*
sheet of paper	la feuille	*lah-fuh-y*
telephone	le téléphone	*luh-tay-lay-fohn*

Dating

- *Es-tu célibataire?* / Are you single?

- *As-tu une petite amie?* / Do you have a girlfriend?

- *Je suis célibataire.* / I'm single.

- *Je suis ici avec mon petit copain.* / I'm here with my boyfriend.

- *Est-ce que tu veux qu'on fasse quelque chose ensemble.* / Would you like to do something together?

- *Est-ce que tu veux aller te balader avec moi?* / Would you like to go for a walk with me?

- *Est-ce que tu es libre demain?* / Are you available tomorrow?

- *Je suis libre demain.* / I'm available tomorrow.

- *Est-ce que tu veux regarder un film.* / Would you like to watch a movie?

- *Est-ce que je peux t'offrir un verre?* / Can I buy you a drink?

- *Est-ce que je te reverrai?* / Will I see you again?

- *Quand peut-on se revoir?* / When can we meet again?

- *Tu es très mignon(ne).* / You're very cute.

- *Tu es très belle.* / You're very beautiful.

- *Tu es formidable.* / You're great.

- *Je t'apprécie beaucoup.* / I like you very much.

- *Je t'aime.* / I love you.

- *Arrêtes de m'appeler.* / Stop calling me.

- *Est-ce que tu vois quelqu'un d'autre?* / Are you seeing someone else?

- *Je ne pense pas que ça va marcher.* / I don't think it's working out.

Exercises

Translate the following words and expressions to French.

A. Everyday Expressions

1. How are you?

2. Very well.

3. See you tomorrow.

4. Hope to see you again.

5. Happy birthday!

6. I'm sorry.

7. Good luck.

8. Good evening!

9. I am twenty-five years old.

10. Are you hungry?

11. I want to take a walk.

12. I'm thirsty.

13. You're wrong.

14. It's sunny.

15. It's running.

B. Family Members

1. grandson

2. grandmother

3. uncle

4. sister

5. cousin (female)

6. niece

7. daughter

8. father

9. aunt

10. wife

C. At Home and Work

1. bathroom

2. door

3. kitchen

4. window

5. garage

6. bed

7. chair

8. mirror

9. desk

10. pillow

11. dishwasher

12. freezer

13. to clean the house

14. to wash the dishes

15. to walk the dog

16. office

17. pen

18. to go to work

19. boss

20. salary

Answers

A.

1. Comment ça va? / Comment allez-vous?

2. Tres bien.

3. À demain.

4. Au plaisir de vous revoir.

5. Bon anniversaire!

6. Je suis désolé.

7. Bonne chance.

8. Bonsoir!

9. J'ai vingt-cinq ans.

10. Tu as faim?

11. Je veux faire une promenade.

12. J'ai soif.

13. Tu as tort.

14. Il fait du soleil.

15. Il pleut.

B.

1. le petit-fils

2. la grand-mère

3. l'oncle

4. la sœur

5. la cousine

6. la nièce

7. la fille

8. le père

9. la tante

10. la femme

C.

1. la salle de bains

2. la porte

3. la cuisine

4. la fenêtre

5. le garage

6. le lit

7. la chaise

8. le miroir

9. le bureau

10. l'oreiller

11. le lave-vaisselle

12. le congélateur

13. faire le ménage

14. laver la vaisselle

15. promener le chien

16. le bureau

17. le stylo

18. aller au travail

19. le patron

20. le salaire

Chapter 7: Shopping

Shopping for Clothes

o *Je cherche ...* / I'm looking for ...

o *Veuillez me montrer?* / Would you please show me?

o *Où puis-je trouver ...?* / Where can I find?

o *Vendez-vous ...?* / Do you sell ...?

o *Combien ça coûte?* / How much does it cost?

o *Je regarde seulement, merci.* / I'm just looking, thanks.

The Clothes

bathing suit	le maillot de bain	*luh-mah-yo-duh-baN*
belt	la ceinture	*lah-saN-tewr*
bikini	le bikini	*luh-bee-kee-nee*
blouse	la blouse	*lah-blooz*
boots	les bottes *f.*	*lay-boht*
bra	le soutien-gorge	*luh-sou-tyahN-gorzh*
cardigan	le gilet	*luh-zhee-luh*
coat	le manteau	*luh-mahN-to*

dress	la robe	*lah-rohb*
gloves	les gants *m.*	*lay-gahN*
hat	le chapeau	*luh-shah-po*
jacket	la veste	*lah-vehst*
jeans	le jean	*luh-zheen*
pajamas	le pyjama	*luh-pee-zhah-mah*
panties	la culotte	*lah-kew-loht*
pants	le pantalon	*luh-pahN-tah-lohN*
raincoat	l'imperméable *m.*	*laN-pehr-may-ahbl*
sandals	les sandales *f.*	*lay-sahN-dahl*
scarf	l'écharpe *f.*	*lay-shahrp*
shirt	la chemise	*lah-shuh-meez*
shoes	les chaussures *f.*	*lay-sho-sewr*
shorts	le short	*luh-shohr*
skirt	la jupe	*lah-zhewp*
sneakers	les tennis	*lay-tay-nees*
socks	les chaussettes *f.*	*lay-sho-seht*
stockings	les bas *m.*	*lay-bah*

suit for men	le complet	*luh-kohN-pleh*
suit for women	le tailleur	*luh-tah-yuhr*
sweater	le pull	*luh-pewl*
tie	la cravate	*lah-krah-vaht*
vest	le gilet	*luh-zhee-leh*

- o *Esc-ce-que je peux l'essayer?* / Can I try it on?

- o *Où sont les cabines?* / Where are the fitting rooms?

- o *Avez-vous de plus grandes tailles?* / Do you have a bigger size?

- o *Avez-vous des tailles plus petites?* / Do you have a smaller size?

- o *Je porte du petit /moyen /grand.* / I wear a small/medium/large.

Materials and Designs

cashmere	en cachemire	*ahN-kahsh-meer*
cotton	en coton	*ahN-koh-tohN*
denim	en jean	*ahN-zheen*
flannel	en flanelle	*ahN-flah-nehl*
lace	en dentelle	*ahN-dahN-tehl*
leather	en cuir	*ahN-kweer*

linen	en lin	*ahN-laN*
satin	en satin	*ahN-sah-taN*
silk	en soie	*ahN-swah*
wool	en laine	*ahN-lehn*
checked	à carreaux	*ah-kah-ro*
in a solid color	uni(e)	*ew-nee*
in herringbone	à chevrons	*ah-shuh-vrohN*
in plaid	en tartan	*ahN-tahr-tahN*
print	imprimé	*ahN-pree-may*
with stripes	à rayures	*ah-rah-yewr*

Colors

o *Avez-vous d'autres couleurs?* / Do you have a different color?

the colors	les couleurs	*lay-koo-luhr*
black	noir	*nwahr*
brown	marron, brun	*mah-rohN, bruhN*
blue	bleu	*bluh*
gray	gris	*gree*
green	vert	*vehr*

pink	rose	*roz*
purple	mauve	*mov*
orange	orange	*oh-rahNzh*
red	rouge	*roozh*
yellow	jaune	*zhon*
white	blanc	*blahN*
beige	beige	*behzh*
sky blue	bleu ciel	*bluh syehl*
navy blue	bleu marine	*bluh mah-reen*
crimson	cramoisi	*krah-mwah-zee*
lavender	lavande	*lah-vahNd*
teal	sarcelle	*sahr-sehl*
light	clair	*klehr*
dark	foncé	*fohN-say*

Shopping for Food

Fruits

apple	la pomme	*lah-pohm*
avocado	l'avocat *m.*	*lah-voh-kah*
banana	la banane	*lah-bah-nahn*

blackcurrant	le cassis	*luh-kah-see*
blueberry	la myrtille	*lah-meer-tee-y*
cherry	la cerise	*lah-suh-reez*
chestnut	la châtaigne	*lah-shah-teh-nyuh*
coconut	la noix de coco	*lah-nwah-duh-koh-ko*
date	la datte	*lah-daht*
fig	la figue	*lah-feeg*
grape	le raisin	*luh-reh-zaN*
grapefruit	le pamplemousse	*luh-pahNpl-moos*
guava	la goyave	*lah-goh-yahv*
kiwi	le kiwi	*luh-kee-wee*
lemon	le citron	*luh-see-trohN*
lime	le citron vert	*luh-see-trohN-vehr*
mango	la mangue	*lah-mahNg-uh*
orange	l'orange *f.*	*loh-rahNzh*
papaya	la papaye	*lah-pah-pahy*
peach	la pêche	*lah-pehsh*

pear	la poire	*lah pwahr*
pineapple	l'ananas *m.*	*lah-nah-nah*
plum	la prune	*lah-prewn*
raspberry	la framboise	*lah-frahN-bwahz*
strawberry	la fraise	*lah-frehz*
tangerine	la mandarine	*lah-mahN-dah-reen*
tomato	la tomate	*lah-toh-maht*
watermelon	la pastèque	*lah-pahs-tehk*

Vegetables

artichoke	l'artichaut *m.*	*lahr-tee-shoh*
asparagus	les asperges *f.*	*lay-zahs-pehrzh*
beet	la betterave	*lah-beht-rahv*
broccoli	le brocoli	*luh-broh-koh-lee*
cabbagge	le chou	*luh-shoo*
carrot	la carotte	*lah-kah-roht*
cauliflower	le chou-fleur	*luh-shoo-fluhr*
celery	le céleri	*luh-sayl-ree*
cucumber	le concombre	*luh-kohN-kohNbr*

corn	le maïs	*luh-mah-ees*
eggplant	l'aubergine *f.*	*lo-behr-zheen*
green beans	les haricots verts	*lay-ah-ree-koh-vehr*
leek	le poireau	*luh-pwah-ro*
lentil	la lentille	*lah-lahN-teel*
lettuce	la laitue	*lah-leh-tew*
mushroom	le champignon	*luh-shahN-pee-nyohN*
onion	l'oignon	*loh-nyohN*
peas	les petits pois *m.*	*lay-puh-tee-pwah*
potato	la pomme de terre	*lah-pohm-duh-tehr*
pumpkin	la citrouille	*lah-see-troo-y*
radish	le radis	*luh-rah-dee*
spinach	les épinards *m.*	*lay-zay-pee-nahr*
squash	la courge	*lah-koorzh*
sweet potato	la patate douce	*lah-pah-taht-doos*
turnip	la rabe	*lah-rahb*
watercress	le cresson	*luh-kreh-sohN*

| zucchini | la courgette | *lah-koor-zhet* |

Condiments, Herbs, and Spices

basil	le basilic	*luh-bah-zee-leek*
bay leaf	la feuille de laurier	*lah-fuhy-duh-loh-ryay*
butter	le beurre	*luh-buhr*
chives	la ciboulette	*lah-see-boo-leht*
condiments	les condiments	*lay-kohn-dee-mahN*
dill	l'aneth *m.*	*lah-neht*
garlic	l'ail *m.*	*lahy*
ginger	le gingembre	*luh-zhaN-zhahNbr*
herbs	les herbes	*lay-zehrb*
horseradish	le raifort	*luh-reh-fohr*
jam	la confiture	*lah-kohN-fee-tewr*
ketchup	le ketchup	*luh-keht-shuhp*
maple syrup	le sirop d'érable	*luh-see-roh-day-rahbl*
mayonnaise	la mayonnaise	*lah-mah-yoh-nehz*
mint	la menthe	*lah-mahNt*
mustard	la moutarde	*lah-moo-tahrd*

oil	l'huile *f.*	*lweel*
oregano	l'origan *m.*	*loh-ree-gahN*
parsley	le persil	*luh-pehr-seel*
pepper	le poivre	*luh-pwahvr*
salt	le sel	*luh-sehl*
tarragon	l'estragon *m.*	*lehs-trah-gohN*
vinegar	le vinaigre	*luh-vee-nehgr*

Meat and Seafoods

meat	la viande	*luh-vyahNd*
beef	le bœuf	*luh-buhf*
chopped meat	la viande hachée	*lah-vyahNd-ah-shay*
cutlet	la côtelette	*lah-kot-leht*
ham	le jambon	*luh-zhahN-bohN*
lamb	l'agneau *m.*	*lah-nyo*
liver	le foie	*luh-fwah*
mutton	le mouton	*luh-moo-tohN*
pork	le porc	*luh-pohr*
prime cut	l'onglet *m.*	*lohN-gleh*

red meat	la viande rouge	*lah-vyahNd-roozh*
roast beef	le rosbif	*luh-rohs-beef*
sausage	les saucisses *f.*	*lay-so-sees*
spareribs	les basses côtes *f.*	*lay-bahs-kot*
veal	le veau	*luh-vo*
chicken	le poulet	*luh-poo-leh*
duck	le canard	*luh-kah-nahr*
turkey	la dinde	*lah-daNd*
venison	la venaison	*lah-vuh-neh-zohN*
breast	la poitrine	*lah-pwah-treen*
leg/thigh	la cuisse	*lah-kwees*
fillet	le filet	*luh-fee-lay*
bass	la perche	*lah-pehrsh*
clam	la palourde	*lah-pah-loord*
crab	le crabe	*luh-krahb*
flounder	le carrelet	*luh-kahr-leh*
grouper	le mérou	*luh-may-roo*
halibut	le flétan	*luh-flay-tahN*
herring	le hareng	*luh-ah-rahN*

lobster	le homard	*luh-oh-mahr*
mackerel	le maquereau	*luh-mahk-ro*
mussel	la moule	*lah-mool*
oyster	l'huître *f.*	*lwee-truh*
red snapper	la perche rouge	*lah-pehrsh-roozh*
salmon	le saumon	*luh-so-mohN*
sardine	la sardine	*lah-sahr-deen*
scallops	les coquilles	*lay-koh-kee-y*
sea bass	le bar	*luh-bahr*
shrimp	la crevette	*lah-kruh-veht*
snail	l'escargot *m.*	*lehs-kahr-go*
squid	le calmar	*luh-kahl-mahr*
trout	la truite	*lah-trweet*
tuna	le thon	*luh tohN*

At the Supermarket

supermarket, grocery store	le supermarché	*luh-soo-pehr-mahr-shay*
aisle	l'allée	*lah-lay*
baby section	les articles pour bébés	*lay-zahr-teekl-poor-bay-bay*

bar code	le code barres	*luh-kohd-bahr*
beverages	les boissons	*lay-bwah-sohN*
canned food	les converves	*lay-kohN-vehrv*
cashier	le caissier	*luh-keh-syay*
checkout	la caisse	*lah-kehs*
dairy section	la crémerie	*lah-kraym-ree*
electrical goods	l'électroménager	*luh-lehk-troh-may-nah-zhay*
frozen food	les produits surgelés	*lay-proh-dwee-sewr-zhuh-lay*
household cleaning products	les produits d'entretien	*lay-proh-dwee-dahN-truh-tyahN*
instant meals	les plat cuisinés	*lay-plah-kwee-zee-neh*
pet food	la nourriture pour animaux	*lah-noo-ree-tewr-poor-ah-nee-mo*
sales, offers	les promotions	*lay-proh-moh-syohN*
scanner	le lecteur optique	*luh-lehk-tuhr-ohp-teek*
shelf	l'étagère	*lay-tah-zhehr*

shopping bag	le sac a provisions	*luh-sahk-ah-proh-vee-zyohN*
shopping basket	le panier	*luh-pah-nyay*
shopping cart	le caddie	*luh-kah-dee*
toiletries	les articles de toilette	*lay-zahr-teekl-duh-twah-leht*

Getting the Right Amount

bag	un sac	*uhN-sahk*
bar	une tablette	*ewn-tah-bleht*
bottle	une bouteille	*ewn-boo-teh-y*
box, can	une boîte	*ewn-bwaht*
dozen	une douzaine	*ewn-doo-zehn*
handful	une poigneé	*ewn-pwah-nyay*
jar	un bocal	*uhN-boh-kahl*
kilogram	un kilo	*uhN-kee-lo*
liter	un litre	*uhN-leetr*
package	un paquet	*uhN-pah-keh*
pair	une paire	*ewn-pehr*
percent	pour cent	*poor-sahN*
percentage	le pourcentage	*luh-poor-sahN-*

		tazh
piece	un morceau	*uhN-mohr-so*
pinch	une pincée	*ewn-paN-say*
pound	une livre	*ewn-leevr*
slice	une tranche	*ewn-trahNsh*
spoonful	une cuillerée	*ewn-kwee-yeh-ray*

Paying

- *Je vais prendre ça.* / I will take this.

- *Où est-ce que je peux payer?* / Where can I pay?

- *Prenez-vous les cartes de crédit?* / Do you accept credit card?

- *Ja paye en liquide.* / I'm paying in cash.

- *J'ai besoin du reçu.* / I need the receipt.

- *Je ne veux pas de sac.* / I don't want a bag.

Exercises

Translate the following words and expressions to French.

A. Clothes

1. coat

2. a cotton dress

3. a leather jacket

4. pants

5. shorts

6. a pair of orange gloves

7. a yellow skirt

8. gray socks

9. a green sweater

10. a blue bathing suit

B. Shopping Expressions

1. Where can I pay?

2. I don't want a bag.

3. I'm paying in cash.

4. I'm looking for a pair of red shoes.

5. Where are the fitting rooms?

C. Shopping for Food

1. banana

2. lemon

3. mango

4. raspberry

5. strawberry

6. beet

7. celery

8. lettuce

9. pumpkin

10. eggplant

11. meat

12. pork

13. chicken

14. lobster

15. shrimp

Answers

A.

1. le manteau

2. une robe en coton

3. un vest en cuir

4. le pantalon

5. le short

6. un paire de gants orange

7. une jupe jaune

8. les chaussettes grises

9. un pull vert

10. un maillot de bain bleu

B.

1. Où est-ce que je peux payer?

2. Je ne veux pas de sac.

3. Ja paye en liquide.

4. Je cherche un paire de chaussures rouges.

5. Où sont les cabines?

C.

1. la banane

2. le citron

3. la mangue

4. la framboise

5. la fraise

6. la betterave

7. le céleri

8. la laitue

9. la citrouille

10. l'aubergine

11. la viande

12. le porc

13. le poulet

14. le homard

15. la crevette

Chapter 8: Travel

Where are You from? Where are You Going? / D'où êtes-vous? Où allez-vous?

The Continents

Africa	l'Afrique	*lah-freek*
Antarctica	l'Antarctique	*lahN-tahrk-teek*
Asia	l'Asie	*lah-zee*
Europe	l'Europe	*lew-rohp*
North America	l'Amérique du Nord	*lah-may-reek-dew-nohr*
Oceania	l'Océanie	*loh-syah-nee*
South America	l'Amérique du Sud	*lah-may-reek-dew-sewd*

Countries and Nationalities

		Nationalities
Algeria	L'Algérie	algérien / algérien
Australia	L'Australie *f.*	australien / australienne
Austria	L'Autriche *f.*	autrichien / autrichienne

Belgium	La Belgique	belge
Brazil	Le Brésil	brésilien / brésilienne
Cambodia	Le Cambodge	cambodgien / cambodgienne
Canada	Le Canada	canadien / canadienne
China	La Chine	chinois / chinoise
Denmark	Le Danemark	danois / danoise
Egypt	L'Égypte *f.*	égyptien / égyptienne
England	L'Angleterre *f.*	anglais / anglaise
Finland	La Finlande	finlandais / finlandaise
France	La France	français / française
Germany	L'Allemagne *f.*	allemand / allemande
Great Britain	La Grande-Bretagne	britannique
Greece	La Grèce	grec / grecque
Hungary	L'Hongrie *f.*	hongrois / hongroise
Iceland	L'Islande *f.*	islandais / islandaise
India	L'Inde *f.*	indien / indienne
Iran	L'Iran *m.*	iranien / iranienne
Ireland	L'Irlande *f.*	irlandais / irlandaise

Israel	L'Israël *m.*	israélien / israélienne
Italy	L'Italie *f.*	italien / italienne
Japan	Le Japon	japonais / japonaise
Mauritius	La Maurice	mauritanien / mauritanienne
Mexico	Le Mexique	mexicain / mexicaine
Morocco	Le Maroc	marocain / marocaine
Netherlands	Les Pays-Bas *m.*	néerlandais / néerlandaise
New Zealand	La Nouvelle-Zélande	néo-zélandais / néo-zélandaise
Norway	La Norvège	norvégien / norvégienne
Poland	La Pologne	polonais / polonaise
Portugal	Le Portugal	portugais / portugaise
Russia	La Russie	russe
Scotland	L'Écosse *f.*	écossais / écossaise
South Korea	La Corée	coréen / coréenne
Spain	L'Espagne *f.*	espagnol / espagnole
Sweden	La Suède	suédois / suédoise
Switzerland	La Suisse	suisse

United States	Les États-Unis	américain / américaine
Vietnam	Le Vietnam	vietnamien / vietnamienne
Zimbabwe	Le Zimbabwe	zimbabwéen / zimbabwéen

- o *Je suis des États-Unis.* / I'm from the USA.

- o *Je suis américain(e).* / I'am American.

- o *Je vais en france.* / I'm going to France.

At the Airport and Inside the Plane

English	French	Pronunciation
airline	la ligne aérienne	*lah-lee-nyuh-ahy-ryehn*
airplane	l'avion	*lah-vyohN*
airport	l'aéroport	*lahy-roh-pohr*
aisle	le couloir	*luh-kool-wahr*
arrival	l'arrivée	*lah-ree-vay*
baggage claim area	les bagages	*lay-bah-gahzh*
bathrooms	les toilettes	*lay-twah-leht*
to board	embarquer	*ahN-bahr-kay*

carry-on luggage	les bagages à main	*lay-bah-gahzh-ah-maN*
cart	le chariot	*luh-shah-ryoh*
check-in counter	le guichet d'embarquement	*luh-gee-sheh-dahN-bahrk-mahN*
crew	l'équipage	*lay-kee-pahzh*
customs	la douane	*lah-doo-ahn*
departure	le départ	*luh-day-pahr*
elevators	les ascenseurs	*lay-zah-sahN-suhr*
emergency exit	la sortie de secours	*lah-sohr-tee-duh-suh-koor*
entrance	l'entrée	*lahN-tray*
exit	la sortie	*lah-sohr-tee*
flight	le vol	*luh-vohl*
gate	la porte	*lah-pohrt*
information	les renseignements	*lay-rahN-seh-nyuh-mahN*
life vest	le gilet de sauvetage	*luh-zhee-leh-duh-sohv-tahzh*
money exchange	le bureau de change	*luh-bew-ro-duh-shahNzh*
passport	le passeport	*luh-pahs-pohr*

passport control	le contrôle des passeports	*luh-kohN-trohl-day-pahs-pohr*
row	le rang	*luh rahN*
seat	la place	*lah-plahs*
seatbelt	la ceinture de sécurité	*lah-saN-tewr-duh-say-kew-ree-tay*
security check	le contrôle de sécurité	*luh-kohN-trohl-duh-say-kew-ree-tay*
takeoff	le décollage	*luh-day-koh-lahzh*
ticket	le billet	*luh-bee-yeh*

Departure and Arrival

o *Je voudrais avoir un siège du côté hublot (couloir), s'il vous plaît.* / I'd like to have a window (aisle) seat, please.

o *Je n'ai rien à déclarer.* / I have nothing to declare.

o *Je vais rester ici une semaine.* / I'll stay here for a week.

o *Je suis juste en transit.* / I'm here in transit.

o *Mes bagages sont manquants.* / My luggage missing.

o *Où puis-je échanger mon argent?* / Where can I exchange my money?

Getting to Your Destination

Travelling by Bus

- *Où est l'arrêt de bus le plus proche?* – Where's the nearest bus stop?

- *Combien coûte un billet?* – How much is the fare?

- *Combien de temps dure le trajet jusqu'à ...?* – How long is the trip to ...?

- *Est-ce que ce bus s'arrête à ...?* – Does this bus stop at ...?

- *Quel est le prochain arrêt?* – What's the next stop?

- *J'aimerai m'arrêter à ...* - I'd like to get off at ...

Travelling by Train

- *un billet simple* – one-way ticket

- *un aller retour* – round-trip ticket

- *train rapide* – express train

- *première classe* – first class

- *deuxième classe* – second class

- *les guichets* – ticket counter

- *un compartiment non fumeurs* – a non-smoking compartment

- *contrôle des tickets* – ticket verification

- *Où est la gare la plus proche?* – Where's the nearest train station?

- *Je voudrais réserver une place.* – I'd like to reserve a seat.

- *De quel quia part-il?* – From which platform does it leave?

- *Est-ce un train direct?* – Is it a direct train?

- *A quelle heure part le train pour …?* – What time does the train for … leave?

Taking the Subway

- *le métro* – subway

- *un abonnemet* – subscription / pass

- *un terminus* – last stop

- *souterrain* – underground

- *Places Prioritaires* – Reserved Seats

- *Où se trouve la station de métro la plus proche?* – Where's the nearest subway station?

- *Quelle est la station?* – What station is this?

- *Quelle est la prochaine station?* – What's the next station?

- *Il reste combien d'arrêts?* – How many more stops are there?

- *Ais-je besoin de changer de train?* – Do I need to change train?

- *Quelle ligne s'arrête à ...?* – Which line goes to ...?

- *Est-ce le bon sens pour aller à ...?* – Is this the right way going to ...?

- *Où est la sortie?* – Where's the exit?

Taking a Taxi

- *Où est l'arrêt de taxi le plus proche?* – Where's the nearest taxi stand?

- *Appelez-moi un taxi, s'il vous plaît.* – Would you please call me a taxi?

- *Pouvez-vous m'emmener à ...?* – Can you take me to ...?

- *Attendez-moi.* – Wait for me.

Renting a Car

- *Je voudrais louer une voiture.* – I'd like to rent a car.

- *Quel est le tarif à la journée/semaine?* – How much does it cost per day/week?

- *Est-ce que ça inclut une assurance?* – Does it include insurance?

- *Quel est le montant de l'assurance?* – How much is the insurance?

- *Qu'est-ce qu'elle prend du diesel ou de l'essence?* – Does the car take diesel or petrol?

- *Acceptez-vous des cartes de crédit?* – Do you accept credit cards?

- *Quan dois-je la rendre?* – When do I have to return it?

- *Voici mon permis de conduire.* – Here's my driving license.

Road and Traffic Signs

- *Bande d'arrêt d'urgence* – Emergency Lane

- *Cédez la Priorité* – Give Way

- *Chaussée glissante* – Slippery Road

- *Deviation* - Detour

- *Entrée* – Entrance

- *Fin de chantier* – End of Roadworks

- *Interdiction de Doubler* – No Overtaking

- *Péage* - Toll

- *Ralentir* – Slow Down

- *Sens Interdit* – No Entry

- *Sens Unique* – One Way

- *Sortie* - Exit

- *Stationnement Interdet / Défense de Stationner* – No Parking

- *Travaux* – Roadworks ahead

At the Hotel

Amenities and Services

English	French	Pronunciation
bar	le bar	*luh-bahr*
bellhop	le bagagiste	*luh-bah-gah-zheest*
concierge	le (la) concierge	*luh-(lah)-kohN-syehrzh*
doorman	le portier	*luh-pohr-tyay*
elevator	l'ascenseur	*lah-sahN-suhr*
maid service	la gouvernante	*lah-goo-vehr-nahNt*
staircase	l'escalier	*lehs-kahl-yay*
swimming pool	la piscine	*lah-pee-seen*
valet parking	l'attendance du garage	*lah-than-dahNs-dew-gah-rahzh*

Note: To avoid confusion, remember that the ground floor of French buildings is called *le rez-de-chaussée* (level with the road). The basement is called *le sous-sol*. The floor above the ground floor is the first floor.

Checking in and Out

- *J'ai une réservation.* / I have a reservation.

- *J'aimerais faire le check-in.* / I'd like to check-in.

- *À quelle heure est le petit déjeuner?* / When is breakfast served?

- *À quelle heure est le check-out?* / What time is the check-out?

- *Quel est le mot de passe wifi?* / What's the wifi password?

- *Est-ce que je peux changer de chambre?* / Can I change room?

- *Pouvez-vous nous conseiller un bon restaurant?* / Can you recommend a good restaurant?

- *Pourriez-vous me réveiller par téléphone à ...* / Could you give me a wake-up call at ...?

- *J'aimerais faire le check-out.* / I'd like to check out.

- *Je voudrais régler mon compte.* / I'd like to pay my bill.

- *J'ai passé un très bon séjour, merci.* / I had a great time, thank you.

Searching for Another Hotel

- *Pouvez-vous me recommander un bon l'hotel?* – Can you recommend a good hotel?

- *J'ai une réservation.* / I don't have a reservation.

- *Avez-vous une chambre libre pour ce soir?* – Do you have a room for tonight?

- *Avez-vous une chambre simple / double / jumeaux?* – Do you have a single / double / twin room?

- *C'est combien la nuit?* / How much is it per night?

- *Je ne sais pas combien de temps je vais rester.* / I don't know how long I'll be staying.

- *Le petit déjeuner est-il inclus?* / Is breakfast included?

- *Y a-t-il une salle de bain?* – Is there en-suite bathroom?

- *Est-ce que je peux la voir?* – May I seet it?

- *Puis-je utiliser la lavarie/cuisine?* – Can I use the laundry/kitchen?

- *Je vais la prendre.* – I'll take it.

The Hotel Room

air conditioning	la climatisation	*lah-klee-mah-tee-zah-syohN*
balcony	un balcon	*uhN-bahl-kohN*
bar of soap	une savonnette	*ewn-saah-voh-neht*
bathroom	une salle de bains	*ewn-sahl-duh-baN*
bathtub	la baignore	*lah-beh-nwar*
bed	le lit	*luh-lee*
blanket	une couverture	*ewn-koo-vehr-tewr*
door	la porte	*lah-pohr*
hair dryer	un sèche-cheveux	*uhN-sehsh-shuh-vuh*
hangers	des cintres	*day-saNtr*

key	une clé	*ewn-klay*
mirror	un miroir	*uhN-mee-rwahr*
pillow	un oreiller	*uhN-noh-reh-yay*
safe	un coffre	*uhN-kohfr*
shower	une douche	*ewn-doosh*
single room	une chambre à un lit	*ewn-shahNbr-ah-uhN-lee*
double room	une chambre à deux lits	*ewn-shahNbr-ah-duh-lee*
sink	le lavabo	*luh-lah-va-boh*
sofa	le canapé	*luh-kah-na-pay*
tissues	des mouchoirs en papier	*day-moo-shwahr-ahN-pah-pyay*
toilet	la toilette	*lah-twa-leht*
a towel	une serviette	*ewn-sehr-vyeht*

Seeing the Sights

o *Qu'est-ce qu'il y a à voir?* What's there to see?

o *Où puis-je acheter une carte?* / Where can I buy a map?

o *À quelle heure ouvre-t-il/ferme-t-il?* / At what time does it open/close?

o *Quel es le tarif?* / What's the admission price?

- *On peut fair des photos?* / Is it okay to take photos?

- *Il me fait un guide qui parle anglais.* / I need an English-speaking guide.

- *Y a-t-il des visites guidées?* / Are there guided tours?

Places to See

English	French	Pronunciation
to the amusement park	au parc d'attractions	*o-pahrk-dah-trahk-syohN*
to the bridge	au pont	*o-pohN*
to the castle	au château	*o-shah-to*
to the cathedral	à la cathédrale	*ah-lah-kah-tay-drahl*
to the church	à l'église	*ah-lay-gleez*
to the flea market	au marché aux puces	*o-mahr-shay-o-pews*
to the fountain	à la fontaine	*ah-lah-fohN-tehn*
to the garden	au jardin	*o-zhahr-daN*
to the lake	au lac	*o-lak*
to the museum	au musée	*o-mew-zay*
to the nightclub	au cabaret	*o-kah-bah-reh*
to the old city (town)	à la vieille ville	*ah-lah-vyay-veel*

to the public square	à la place	*ah-lah-plahs*
to the river bank	à la rive	*ah-lah-reev*
to the ruins	aux ruines	*o-rween*
to the tower	à la tour	*ah-lah-toor*
to the zoo	au zoo	*o-zo*

Asking for Directions

- *Est-ce que vous savez où ...?* – Do you know where the ... is?

- *Comment y aller?* / How do I get there?

- *Est-ce loin?* / How far is it?

- *Excusez-moi. Je me suis perdu. Pouvez-vous m'aider?* / Excuse me. I'm lost. Can you help me?

What You May Hear

- *C'est loin.* / It's far.

- *C'est près d'ici.* / It's near.

- *Tournez à gauche (droite).* – Turn left (right).

- *Prenez la rue / le boulevard ...* - Take ... street.

- *Aller en taxi.* – Go by taxi.

Dining Out

- *Bonjour. J'ai une réservation pour deux sous le nom de ...* / Hello. I have a reservation for two under the name of ...

- *Avez-vous une table pour ...* / Do you have a table for ...

- *La carte, s'il vous plaît.* / The menu, please.

- *Qu'est-ce que vous recommandez?* / What do you recommend?

- *Quelle est las spécialité de la maison?* / What's the house specialty?

- *Je voudrais ...* / I would like ...

What You May Hear

- *Qu'est-ce que vous voulez commander?* / What would you like to order?

- *Vous avez choisi?* / Have you decided?

- *Qu'est-ce que je vous sers?* / What can I get you?

Table Setting

bowl	le bol	*luh-bohl*
cup	la tasse	*lah-tahs*
dinner plate	l'assiette *f.*	*lah-syeht*
fork	la fourchette	*lah-foor-sheht*

glass	le verre	*luh-vehr*
knife	le couteau	*luh-koo-to*
menu	la carte	*lah-kahrt*
napkin	la serviette	*lah-sehr-vyeht*
pepper shaker	la poivrière	*lah-pwah-vree-yehr*
salt shaker	la salière	*lah-sahl-yehr*
saucer	la soucoupe	*lah-soo-koop*
soup dish	l'assiette à soupe	*lah-syeht-ah-soop*
soup spoon	la cuiller à soupe	*lah-kwee-yeah-ah-soop*
tablecloth	la nappe	*lah-nahp*
teaspoon	la cuiller	*lah-kwee-yehr*
wine glass	le verre à vin	*luh-vehr-ah-vaN*

Food and Drink

aioli	*ah-yoh-lee*	garlic-flavored mayonnaise
bercy	*behr-see*	a fish or meat sauce
crécy	*kray-see*	carrots
daube	*dohb*	a stew, usually beef
Florentine	*floh-rahN-teen*	spinach

forestière	*foh-rehs-tyehr*	wild mushrooms
parmentier	*pahr-mahN-tyay*	potatoes
périgourdine	*pay-ree-goor-deen*	truffles
Provençale	*proh-vahN-sahl*	a vegetable garnish
une salade	*ewn-sah-lahd*	salad, lettuce
les hors-d'œuvres	*lay ohr-duhvr*	appetizers
escargots à la bourguignonne	*ehs-kahr-go-ah-lah-boor-gee-nyohn*	snails in garlic-herb butter
pâté	*pah-tay*	pureed liver served in a loaf
foie gras	*fwah-grah*	fresh goose or duck liver
les soups	*lay-soop*	soups
la bouillabaisse	*lah-boo-yah-behs*	seafood stew
le consommé	*luh-kohN-soh-may*	clear broth
la soupe à l'oignon	*lah-soop-ah loh-nyohN*	onion soup
le velouté	*luh-vuh-loo-tay*	creamy soup

les viandes	*lay-vyahnd*	meats
le bifteck	*luh-beef-tehk*	steak
le chateaubriand	*luh-shah-to-bree-yahN*	a porterhouse steak
la côte de boeœuf	*lah-kot-duh-buhf*	prime rib
le rosbif	*luh-rohs-beef*	roast beef
le dessert	*luh-dee-sehr*	dessert
une bavaroise	*ewn-bah-vahr-wahz*	Bavarian cream
une bombe	*ewn-bohNb*	ice cream with different flavors
une glace	*ewn-glahs*	ice cream
un yaourt	*uhN-yah-oort*	yogurt
le vin	*luh-vaN*	wine
le vin rouge	*luh-vaN-roozh*	red wine
le vin blanc	*luh-vaN-blahN*	white wine
le champagne	*luh-shahN-pah-nyuh*	champagne

Drinking

- *Je voudrais ... /* I'd like ...

    - *une bière (pression)* – a (draught) beer

    - *une bière anglaise* – an ale

    - *une bouteille de vin* – a bottle of wine

    - *un cognac* – a brandy

    - *un martini* – a martini

    - *une vodka* – a vodka

- *Sans glaçons s'il vous plaît.* – No ice, please.

- *Cul sec!* – Bottoms up!

- *Santé!* – Cheers!

- *Une autre tournée, s'il vous plaît.* – Another round, please.

- *On va prendre des shooters. /* We're going to take shots.

- *Je suis saoul(e).* – I'm drunk.

Health and Emergency

Calling for Help

- *Aidez-moi! /* Help me!

- *Ja besoin d'un docteur qui parle Anglais. /* I need a doctor who can speak English.

- o *J'ai eu un accident. Je besoin d'une ambulance.* / I've had an accident. I need an ambulance.

- o *C'est une urgence.* / It's an emergency.

- o *Appelez un docteur!* / Call a doctor!

Visiting a Doctor

- o *Où est l'hôpital le plus proche?* / Where's the nearest hospital?

- o *Je ne me sens pas bien.* / I'm not feeling well.

- o *Je suis malade.* / I'm sick.

- o *Ça fait mal ici.* / It hurts here.

- o *J'ai fais mes rappels.* / I have had vaccinations.

- o *Je fais une allergie.* / I have an allergy.

Parts of the Body

arm	le bras	*luh-brah*
back	le dos	*luh-do*
chest	la poitrine	*lah-pwah-treen*
ear	l'oreille *f.*	*loh-reh-y*
elbow	le coude	*luh-kood*
eye	l'œil *m.*	*luhy*
eyes	les yeux	*lay-zyuh*

face	la figure	*lah-fee-gewr*
finger	le doigt	*luh-dwah*
foot	le pied	*luh-pyay*
hand	la main	*lah-maN*
head	la tête	*lah-teht*
heart	le cœur	*luh-kuhr*
hip	la hanche	*lah-ahNsh*
kidney	le rein	*luh-raN*
knee	le genou	*luh-zhuh-nou*
leg	la jambe	*lah-zhahNb*
lip	la lèvre	*lah-lehvr*
lung	le poumon	*luh-poo-mohN*
mouth	la bouche	*lah-boosh*
neck	le cou	*luh-koo*
nose	le nez	*luh-nay*
shoulder	l'épaule	*lay-pohl*
stomach	l'estomac	*leh-stoh-mah*
throat	la gorge	*lah-gohrzh*
toe	l'orteil *m.*	*lohr-they*

tongue	la langue	*lah-lahNg*
tooth	la dent	*lah-dahN*
wrist	le poignet	*luh-pwah-nyeh*

- *J'ai mal à la poitrine.* / My chest hurts.

- *J'ai mal à la gorge.* / I have a sore throat.

- *J'ai mal de tête terrible.* / I have a terrible headache.

Drugstore Items

absorbent cotton	du coton	*dew-koh-tohN*
alcohol	de l'alcool	*duh-lahl-kohl*
antacid	un anti-acide	*uhN-nahN-tee-ah-seed*
antihistamine	un antihistaminique	*uhN-nahN-tee-ees-tah-mee-neek*
antiseptic	un antiseptique	*uhN-nahN-tee-sehp-teek*
anti-dandruff shampoo	du shampooing anti-pellicules	*dew-shahN-pwaN-ahN-tee-peh-lee-kewl*
aspirins	des aspirines	*day-zah-spee-reen*
Band-aid	un pansement adhésif	*uhN-pahNs-mahN-ahd-ay-zeef*

bottle	un biberon	*uhN-beeb-rohN*
brush	une brosse	*ewn-brohs*
comb	un peigne	*uhN-peh-nyuh*
cough drops	des pastilles contre la toux *f.*	*day-pah-stee-y-kohNtr-lah-too*
cough syrup	le sirop contre la toux	*luh-see-roh-kohNtr-lah-too*
deodorant	du déodorant	*dew-day-oh-doh-rahN*
diapers	des couches	*day-koosh*
eye drops	du collyre	*dew-koh-leer*
gauze pads	des bandes de gaze *f.*	*day-bahnd-duh-gahz*
ice pack	une vessie de glace	*ewn-veh-see-duh-glahs*
laxative	un laxatif	*uhN-lahk-sah-teef*
mouthwash	de l'eau dentifrice *f.*	*duh-lo-dahN-tee-frees*
nail clippers	un coupe-ongles	*uhN-koop-ohNgl*
pacifier	une sucette	*ewn-sew-seht*
safety pins	des épingles de sûreté *f.*	*day-zay-paNgl-duh-sewr-tay*
sanitary	des serviettes	*day-sehr-vyeht-ee-*

napkins	hygiéniques *f.*	*zhyay-neek*
shaving cream	de la crème à raser	*duh-lah-krehm-ah-rah-zay*
sleeping pills	des somnifères *m.*	*day-sohm-nee-fehr*
soap bar	une savonnette	*ewn-sah-voh-neht*
suntan lotion	de la lotion solaire	*dew-lah-loh-syohN-soh-lehr*
tampons	des tampons périodiques	*day-tahN-pohN-pay-ree-oh-deek*
thermometer	un thermomètre	*uhN-tehr-moh-mehtr*
tissues	des mouchoirs en papier *m.*	*day-moosh-wahr-ahN-pah-pyay*
toothbrush	une brosse à dents	*ewn-brohs-ah-dahN*
toothpaste	de la pâte dentifrice	*duh-lah-paht-dahN-tee-frees*
vitamins	des vitamines *f.*	*day-vee-tah-meen*
wound bandages	des pansements *m.*	*day-pahNs-mahN*

Exercises

A. At the Airport

1. airport

2. check-in counter

3. flight

4. gate

5. baggage claim area

6. cart

7. aisle

8. I'd like to have a window seat.

9. I'll stay here for a month.

10. Where can I exchange my money?

B. Getting Where You're Going

1. one-way ticket

2. subway

3. Slow Down

4. No Parking

5. How much is the fare?

6. I'd like to reserve a seat.

7. What's the next stastion?

8. Wait for me.

9. I'd like to rent a car.

10. Does it include insurance?

C. At the Hotel

1. elevator

2. swimming pool

3. single room

4. safe

5. key

6. I have a reservation.

7. What time is the check-out?

8. Do you have a room for tonight?

9. Is there en-suite bathroom?

10. Is breakfast included?

D. Seeing the Sights

1. to the castle

2. to the lake

3. to the cathedral

4. to the tower

5. to the ruins

6. What's there to see?

7. Do you know where the museum is?

8. How do I get there?

9. Are there guided tours?

10. At what time does it close?

E. Dining Out

1. dinner plate

2. wine glass

3. steak

4. an ice cream

5. appetizers

6. The menu, please.

7. I'd like some seafood stew.

8. Do you have a table for three?

9. Cheers!

10. I'd like a bottle of wine.

F. Health and Emergency.

1. my stomach

2. my ears

3. my hands

4. aspirins

5. antihistamine

6. Help me!

7. It's an emergency.

8. I'm not feeling well.

9. I have an allergy.

10. My chest hurts.

Answers

A.

1. l'aéroport

2. le guichet d'embarquement

3. le vol

4. la porte

5. les bagages

6. le chariot

7. le couloir

8. Je voudrais avoir un siège du côté hublot.

9. Je vais rester ici un mois.

10. Où puis-je échanger mon argent?

B.

1. un billet simple

2. le métro

3. Ralentir

4. Défense de Stationner / Stationnement Interdet

5. Combien coûte un billet?

6. Je voudrais réserver une place.

7. Quelle est la prochaine station?

8. Attendez-moi.

9. Je voudrais louer une voiture.

10. Est-ce que ça inclut une assurance?

C.

1. l'ascenseur

2. la piscine

3. une chambre à un lit

4. un coffre

5. une clé

6. J'ai une réservation.

7. À quelle heure est le check-out?

8. Avez-vous une chambre libre pour ce soir?

9. Y a-t-il une salle de bain?

10. Le petit déjeuner est-il inclus?

D.

1. au château

2. au lac

3. à la cathédrale

4. à la tour

5. aux ruines

6. Qu'est-ce qu'il y a à voir?

7. Est-ce que vous savez où se trouve le musée?

8. Comment y aller?

9. Y a-t-il des visites guidées?

10. À quelle heure ferme-t-il?

E.

1. l'assiette

2. le verre à vin

3. le bifteck

4. une glace

5. les hors-d'œuvres

6. La carte, s'il vous plaît.

7. Je voudrais des bouillabaisse.

8. Avez-vous une table pour trois?

9. Santé!

10. Je voudrais une bouteille de vin.

F.

1. mon estomac

2. mes oreilles

3. mes mains

4. des aspirines

5. un antihistaminique

6. Aidez-moi.

7. C'est une urgence.

8. Je ne me sens pas bien.

9. Je fais une allergie.

10. J'ai mal à la poitrine.

Conclusion

I'd like to thank you and congratulate you for transiting my lines from start to finish.

I hope this book was able to help you learn the basics of and communicate in French or improve your understanding of the French language.

The next step is to practice what you've learned and incorporate French into your daily life. Join online communities and forums. Find someone who can speak French fluently and converse with them. Talk to them as often as you can even when you're not yet confident with your skills. The only thing that can happen when you make mistakes is that your errors will be corrected.

Learn a certain number of words everyday to expand your vocabulary. Aim to know the names of all the things that you regularly encounter in and out of your home and workplace. Change the language setting of your smartphone to French. Watch movies or TV shows and read blogs in French. Not only will you learn new words; your ears will get used to the sound of spoken French. You'll also become familiar with how it's'used colloquially so you won't sound like you came straight out of a French learning textbook.

Dedicate a few minutes of your time each day learning French. Practice every chance you got and soon you'll become fluent in French.

I wish you the best of luck!

CPSIA information can be obtained
at www.ICGtesting.com
Printed in the USA
BVHW011030220321
602886BV00020B/975

9 781801 699723